Marketing Urban Mass Transit

A Comparative Study of Management Strategies

Marketing Urban Mass Transit

A Comparative Study of Management Strategies

Lewis M. Schneider

Assistant Professor of Business Administration
Harvard University

Division of Research
Graduate School of Business Administration
Harvard University
Boston • 1965

It is a policy of the Harvard Business School to have selected theses, written by doctoral candidates in the School, published by the Division of Research. This study is based on the thesis submitted by Mr. Schneider in partial fulfillment of the requirements of the degree of Doctor of Business Administration, and it is published in accordance with that policy.

Library of Congress Catalog Card No. 65–13254
Printed in the United States of America

Foreword

Professor Schneider has written a much needed book. It deals with an activity which has suffered too long from the application of two extreme viewpoints: management concentration on the "production-oriented" operating problems of a transit system and student concentration on discovering how people "should" use a transit system, not on how they want to use one. Professor Schneider's focus is on the broad problems of management; he wisely looks at urban transit companies as organizations whose communities will benefit by having the best current management practices applied to running that particular kind of "business." His study, by emphasizing men and strategies as well as machines, restores some balance to a literature that has stressed that money and technology alone will solve the urban transport problem.

It is particularly valuable in showing how market research, product planning, pricing, and promotion should be combined to design a variety of "packages" to appeal to different segments of the traveling public.

Lastly, Professor Schneider's discussion of formal organization in the transit industry, it seems to me, makes a major contribution. Over all, his message is that of a student of business administration rather than that of an economist, an urban planner, or a civil engineer. It is long overdue.

This study was undertaken as a doctoral thesis at this School. Its publication by the Division of Research was supported in part by an allocation of funds contributed by The Associates of the Harvard Business School.

Boston, Massachusetts
December 1964

GEORGE P. BAKER
Dean

Preface

The author is indebted to many individuals for their interest, cooperation, encouragement, and guidance during the course of this study. He recognizes that the brief words of acknowledgment which follow have two shortcomings; they cannot list all the individuals who helped him during his research, nor can they convey fully the sense of appreciation he feels.

This book is essentially a shortened version of the author's doctoral thesis, "Management Policy in a Distressed Industry: A Study of Urban Mass Transit," which was written during 1962–1963. He would first like to thank the members of his thesis committee: Dean George P. Baker, Professor Paul W. Cherington, Professor Paul W. Cook, and Professor John R. Meyer for their guidance, comments, and encouragement. He would particularly like to single out Professor Cherington, who bore the brunt of reading the manuscript in its formative stages, and guided the author during occasional moments of confusion and chaos.

The field trips which produced much of the factual data for the thesis and this book were made possible by a fellowship granted by the Ford Foundation. Of course the conclusions, opinions, and other statements in this study are those of the author and are not necessarily those of the Ford Foundation.

The author is grateful to the American Transit Association, especially George W. Anderson, its executive vice-president, for its cooperation in securing responses to the questionnaire, supplying statistical data, and approving the methodology of the study.

Similarly, he acknowledges the time and effort contributed by officials of the transit companies visited during the development of the case studies. These men included: Donald C. Hyde and George Inhat, Cleveland Transit System; C. M. Gilliss, Cone T. Bass, Robert Korach, and E. R. Gerlach, Los Angeles Metropolitan Transit Authority (soon to be absorbed by the Southern California Rapid Transit District); Robert H. Stier, George L. Hamilton, and Harold C. Juram, Philadelphia Transportation Company; Walter J. McCarter, L. M. Traiser, C. B. North, and L. C. Dutton, Chicago Transit Authority; and Thomas J. McLernon, E. B. Myott, and Michael J. Powell, Metropolitan Transit Authority (now Massachusetts Bay Transportation Authority). The author hopes that the industry officials to whom he talked sensed he favors strong urban mass transit systems and is extremely sympathetic to the industry's problems. Therefore he asks that they read any conclusions or recommendations which imply weaknesses in existing practices in a spirit of constructive criticism.

Professor Bertrand Fox read the thesis and the revised manuscript and made several suggestions for improvements, which were readily adopted by the author. Miss Ruth Norton guided the book through to publication with remarkable patience. Mrs. Nina Dolben prepared the index and helped in the arduous job of proofreading the manuscript. The task of typing both the thesis and the revised manuscript was borne cheerfully and competently by Miss Dorcas Holden.

Finally, the author gratefully thanks his wife for her patience, understanding, willingness to discuss the study, and encouragement during the thesis stage (when her "dining area" was transformed into an office), and the subsequent year when weekends were devoted to revising the thesis for publication.

Although the author acknowledges the help provided by each of the above individuals, the responsibility for the accuracy of the facts, the conclusions, and recommendations of this study remains his alone.

LEWIS M. SCHNEIDER

Belmont, Massachusetts
October, 1964

Contents

Contents

Tables and Figures

Maps

CHAPTER 1

Introduction

The Mass Transportation Problem

There is little doubt that the problem of transporting persons and goods in our urban areas is one of the most frustrating our nation faces. We stand on the verge of enormous technological advances which will enable us to travel at supersonic speeds to distant planets. Yet, twice each twenty-four hours, millions of persons battle traffic congestion at speeds more reminiscent of pioneers in their covered wagons. Traffic congestion is not a new phenomenon. Crowds and teeming streets have been the trademark of cities for thousands of years. But new methods of transportation have changed the nature of congestion.

Fifty years ago traffic congestion meant pedestrians, wagons, carriages, and the thriving symbol of public transportation: the streetcar. Today, in most cities the urban transportation scene is dominated by private transportation, and the words "traffic jam" are synonomous with endless lines of automobiles clogging expressways and parking lots.

The automobile has freed the urban traveler from the restrictive routes and schedules of public mass transportation and has thus made possible the flight to the suburbs by homeowners, business, and industry. At the same time, in our largest cities the automobile-expressway-parking lot system has been unable to accommodate the heavy volumes of suburbia–core-city traffic needed to sustain high-density core-city activity. This performance failure has been a contributing factor to the decline of the core city and accelerated the growth of the suburbs.

Many planners and public officials have now concluded that our urban areas must possess a strong, balanced private and public transportation system, and have therefore recommended improvements in mass transportation facilities together with continued highway construction. For example, President John F. Kennedy in his 1962 Transportation Message to Congress summarized the importance of mass transportation in these words:

> To conserve and enhance values in existing urban areas is essential. But at least as important are steps to promote economic efficiency and livability in areas of future development. In less than 20 years we can expect well over half of our expanded population to be living in 40 great urban complexes. Many smaller places will also experience phenomenal growth. The ways that people and goods can be moved in these areas will have a major influence on their structure, on the efficiency of their economy, and on the availability for social and cultural opportunities they can offer their citizens. Our national welfare therefore requires the provision of good urban transportation with the properly balanced use of private vehicles and modern mass transport to help shape as well as serve urban growth.[1]

His successor, Lyndon B. Johnson, echoed these words in his 1964 State of the Union Message: "We must help obtain more modern mass transit within our communities as well as low cost transportation between them."[2] On January 27, 1964, he spoke out in favor of President Kennedy's mass transit aid bill and asked for "the proper mixture of good highways and mass transit facilities . . . to permit safe, efficient movement of people and goods in our metropolitan centers."[3]

[1] U.S. Congress, House, Committee of the Whole House on the State of the Union, *The Transportation System of Our Nation; Message from the President of the United States,* 87th Cong., 2d Sess., 1962, House Doc. 384, p. 9.

[2] *Congressional Quarterly Weekly Report,* XXII (Week ending January 10, 1964), p. 47.

[3] *Congressional Quarterly Weekly Report,* XXII (Week ending January 31, 1964), p. 237.

But another group of writers believes strongly that efforts to stimulate use of mass transit will be futile. They contend that the urbanites have displayed an overwhelming desire to travel by automobile, and will continue to do so.[4] The following two quotes best summarize what might be called the pessimistic viewpoint on mass transit:

> . . . neither economic analysis nor transportation history suggests a return to public transportation on a scale which would be decisive.[5]   . . . . .
>
> The automobile has exploded metropolis open, and no amount of public transit will jam it back together again. The automobile looks like an unbeatable invention for circulating people from low-density communities to low-density activities of all kinds.[6]

Regardless of their opinions on the future of urban mass transit, all writers have agreed that it has been playing a diminishing role in the movement of persons in urban areas. All statistical indicators seem to have established the industry as distressed; characterized by declining demand, rising costs, low return on investment, and an inability to raise capital from private sources for modernization.

Largely because of this poor financial performance, many of the nation's most important urban mass transit companies have undergone a transition from private to public ownership, either as quasi-public agencies (transit authorities which cannot levy taxes, but can issue revenue bonds) or tax-supported public operations. In turn, several of the quasi-public mass transit

[4] See John R. Meyer, John F. Kain, and Martin Wohl, "Technology and Urban Transportation—A Report Prepared for the White House Panel on Civilian Technology" (Cambridge: By the authors, mimeographed, 1962), pp. i-x. [Hereafter cited as Meyer et al.] Wilbur Smith & Associates, *Future Highways and Urban Growth* (New Haven: Wilbur Smith & Associates, 1961), p. x. [Hereafter cited as Smith & Associates.] Harry A. Williams, *Just Who is Trying to Ruin Our Cities?* (Detroit: Automobile Manufacturers Association, 1962), p. 7.

[5] Wilfred Owen, *The Metropolitan Transportation Problem* (Washington: Brookings, 1956), p. 253. [Hereafter cited as Owen.]

[6] Francis Bello, "The City and the Car," *The Exploding Metropolis*, ed. The Editors of *Fortune* (Garden City: Doubleday, 1957), p. 56.

authorities have discovered that they can no longer raise needed
funds through revenue bonds, and are attempting to get direct
and indirect financial support from the communities, states, and
federal government. If these unfavorable cost-revenue trends
continue, the industry will be unable to meet operating expenses,
much less capital charges, and will either disappear, receive
subsidies under private operation, or function as a tax-supported
sector of local or regional government.[7]

Existing Urban Mass Transit Studies

In view of the importance of urban mass transportation and
its present financial straits, it is not surprising that the industry
has been the subject of many recent studies. These include:
(a) urban and regional transportation studies, which recommend
a comprehensive system of highways and mass transportation
facilities based on an analysis of forecasted land use and trip
patterns;[8] (b) analyses of different methods of financing and
organizing mass transportation companies;[9] (c) government or
private sponsored surveys of the over-all national urban mass
transportation problem;[10] (d) academic efforts to develop equa-

[7] For a fascinating history of one such component of the domestic trans-
portation industry which did in fact disappear, see George W. Hilton and John
F. Due, *The Electric Interurban Railways in America* (Stanford: Stanford
University, 1960).

[8] An analysis of 23 such studies can be found in Richard M. Zettel and
Richard R. Carll, *Summary Review of Major Metropolitan Area Transportation Studies in the United States* (Berkeley: University of California Institute
of Transportation and Traffic Engineering, 1962).

[9] For example, see Advisory Commission on Intergovernmental Relations,
*Intergovernmental Responsibilities for Mass Transportation Facilities and
Services in Metropolitan Areas* (Washington: By the Commission, 1961), and
Metropolitan Rapid Transit Commission, *Metropolitan Rapid Transit
Financing*. A Report Prepared by William Miller (New York: By the Com-
mission, 1957).

[10] See Owen; Smith & Associates; Meyer et. al.; U.S. Congress, Senate,
Committee on Interstate and Foreign Commerce, Special Study Group on
Transportation Policies in the United States, *National Transportation
Policy; Preliminary Draft of a Report*, 87th Cong., 1st Sess., 1961, pp. 582–
646, hereafter cited under its popular title, *Doyle Report;* and American

tions for predicting travel and mass transit use;[11] (e) feasibility studies of mass transportation (particularly rapid transit) projects financed in part by the Housing and Home Finance Agency; and (f) technical monographs and reports on new forms of transit equipment and fixed facilities.[12]

There is little question that these studies have greatly increased our understanding of the demand for urban mass transportation, and the cost and service implications of meeting this demand by different transportation technologies. Yet, in the author's opinion, these studies have been deficient in failing to analyze the importance of transit management *per se* in the urban transportation picture.

Scope of This Study

This is a study of management in a distressed industry: the administrators of urban mass transit companies. More specifically, this study is focused on the problem of marketing urban mass transit. This emphasis on marketing is deliberate. The author will develop the importance of marketing in three steps.

Municipal Association, *The Collapse of Commuter Service* (Washington: American Municipal Association, 1959). [Hereafter cited as *Collapse of Commuter Service*.]

[11] Of interest are Seminar Research Bureau, *Studies of Urban Transportation, Travel in the Boston Region 1959–1980* (Chestnut Hill: Boston College, 1960–1961); B. V. Martin, F. W. Memmott, A. J. Bone, *Principles and Techniques of Predicting Future Demand for Urban Area Transportation* (Cambridge: Massachusetts Institute of Technology School of Engineering, 1963), especially p. 122; Walter Y. Oi and Paul Shuldiner *An Analysis of Urban Travel Demands* (Chicago: Northwestern University, 1962); and Stanley L. Warner, *Stochastic Choice of Mode in Urban Travel: A Study in Binary Choice* (Chicago: Northwestern University, 1962).

[12] See various issues of *Railway Age, Metropolitan Transportation,* and Institute for Rapid Transit, *Newsletter.* Two recent monographs on the subject are Donald S. Berry, George W. Blomme, Paul Shuldiner, and John H. Jones, *The Technology of Urban Transportation* (Chicago: Northwestern University, 1963); and A. Scheffer Lang and Richard M. Soberman, *Urban Rail Transit* (Cambridge: The Joint Center for Urban Studies of the Massachusetts Institute of Technology and Harvard University, 1964). [Hereafter cited as Lang and Soberman.]

The first will be to outline the adverse patronage and financial trends which confront the industry. Then a close look will be taken at the environment in which transit decision making takes place. A distinction will be made between indirect external pressures, over which management has relatively little control, and direct external pressures. A strategy will be defined as a set of policies planned and implemented by management in response to each of these direct pressures. Finally, what appear to be the most important management internal strategies will be analyzed. These strategies include labor relations, recruiting, research and development, finance, and marketing. The author will assert that marketing emerges as particularly significant, for the solution to the industry's problems hinges on increased patronage, and marketing is the only strategy area which has a direct impact on consumer demand.

Having established the importance of marketing strategy, the study proceeds to analyze the industry's marketing practices with four major questions in mind: (1) In terms of patronage and profits, how successful have different marketing strategies been? (2) What conclusions can be drawn as to the strengths and weaknesses of transit management's marketing strategies? (3) What is the importance of the interrelationship between marketing and political strategy? (4) How does formal organization affect the success or failure of marketing strategy? The first of the study questions is straightforward, but the remaining ones warrant further treatment briefly in this introductory chapter.

The Evaluation of Transit Management's Marketing Strategies

Marketing strategy is defined as the set of pricing, market research, promotion, and product planning policies designed to stimulate the patronage of mass transit and in the process generate or maintain an adequate profit. This study analyzes marketing strategy with the following questions in mind. Does the industry implement policies consistent with the concept of integrated marketing strategies or are the policies uneven or inconsistent? Should different strategies be designed to attract different classes of riders? What factors might be more strongly considered in the planning and implementation of future kinds of service?

The Interrelationship Between Marketing and Political Strategy

In addition to focusing on the decisions of transit management, this study investigates more closely than many recent treatments of the urban transit problem the political environment in which transit functions. The analysis of the external pressures and internal strategy areas evident in the transit decision-making process will clarify the increasingly important roles of government promotion, regulation, and pressure. Should marketing strategy take a different form in view of the importance of government? How can marketing reinforce political strategy? Answers to these questions may well determine the industry's ability to finance vitally needed capital projects.

The Question of Formal Organization

Perhaps the most important variable in transit management's ability to market its product is the quality of its personnel and the manner in which authority and responsibility are delegated for the marketing task. Does the existing formal organization of a transit company lend itself to effective marketing? If not, what kinds of improvements can be made? Might not new patterns of formal organization aid in attracting new managerial talent to the industry, thereby easing the recruiting problem?

Limitations of This Study

Having discussed what this work hopes to accomplish, it would be well to consider briefly topics which are beyond the scope of this study. The author does not attempt to answer the question of whether transit should receive subsidies. This would entail a traditional welfare economics type of analysis replacing "revenues" and "expenses" as defined by the accountant with social costs and benefits of mass transit versus the highway system. In the author's opinion, transit revenues should be sufficient to cover at least total operating expenses (all costs except fixed charges and depreciation).

Nor does this work contain any recommendations as to the appropriate form of financial organization for mass transit companies. Such an analysis would necessitate evaluating a spectrum of possibilities, ranging from private enterprise through quasi-public municipal and state authorities, to tax-supported transit districts. Data, however, are presented which might be of interest to others doing research on this important public policy question.

Finally, the author does not attempt to answer the urban planning question of the optimal balance between private automobiles and mass transit. Rather than having planners dictate such a balance to the community, the author would prefer to see the transit industry market its product in a manner which generates community support for increased public transport facilities.

Methodology and Organization

Sources of Information

This study draws on the literature cited earlier, case studies and interviews obtained from field research, and a questionnaire. Early in the author's research, it was found that a few large companies dominated the activity of the transit industry. A basic sample of twelve companies was identified for analysis. As will be discussed in Chapter 2, the author felt it would be unwise to dwell at length on the problems of the New York City Transit Authority, the largest of the sample companies.

The case studies were written during field trips to five of the sample cities during the late summer of 1962. The major transit companies in these cities—Philadelphia, Pennsylvania; Los Angeles, California; Chicago, Illinois; Cleveland, Ohio; and Boston, Massachusetts—were chosen to present a spectrum ranging from private enterprise (Philadelphia) through financially autonomous transit authorities in various stages of development, to Boston, whose transit system since 1918 has operated under both private and public enterprise with provisions for assessing deficits on the cities and towns served by the company. In addition to interviews with the chief administrative officer and his staff, the author also talked to at least one member of the press in each city, to obtain a better picture of the external pressures, as well as the public's view of the transit company. The complete case studies can be found in the author's doctoral thesis, but because of space limitations they are included in summary form only in this book.

The questionnaire is included as an Appendix to this book. It was originally sent to the chief administrative officer of the twelve sample companies. Six of the twelve, five public and one private, returned the completed questionnaire. In order to achieve a better balance between public and private companies, the author then sent questionnaires to the next eight largest cities. Three additional responses, each from private companies, were received, bringing the sample total to nine of twenty: five public and four private. The importance of the nine responses is seen in the fact that these few companies accounted for 44% of the revenues and 45% of the revenue passengers of the domestic transit companies in 1961.

Outline of the Book

Chapters 2 to 4 draw heavily from the literature, questionnaire, and field trip interviews to present a description of the transit industry—history, financial condition, demand for its service, and formal organization—and an outline of the external pressures and internal strategy decisions confronting management. The analysis indicates the precarious financial position of the industry, and the importance of marketing and political strategies in meeting the direct and indirect external pressures.

Chapters 5 and 6 present and analyze eight case studies, augmented by the questionnaire and the literature. Chapter 5 compares four expressway bus operations, and Chapter 6 reports four investments in rail rapid transit. In each chapter, the analysis focuses on management's marketing and political strategies and the problem of formal organization. Chapter 7 contains a summary of the study and the author's recommendations.

Importance of This Study

Timeliness

It is almost ironic to note that as the financial problems of the industry intensify, the transit industry stands at the possible threshold of a dramatic rennaissance. The $1 billion San Francisco Bay Area rapid transit system is now in the construction stage. Its promotional literature promises a new image of mass transportation embodying speed, comfort, convenience, and safety. In addition, almost daily, the public is bombarded by glowing reports of exotic forms of mass transportation including monorails, "duorails," hydro-foils, transit expressways, etc. The recently approved $375 million federal mass transportation capital aid program should stimulate investment in these kinds of facilities and equipment. Admittedly technological improvements in mass transportation are important and warrant continued research and development. But, it is equally, if not at this time more, important to reassert the role of men and their strategies as well as machines. In short, it appears to the author that the challenge to the administrators in the urban mass transportation industry is to exploit technological advances, make transit attractive and desirable to the public, and thereby remove the stigma of unpleasantness which has haunted the industry almost since its inception.

Information

Although the case studies were written two years ago, they contain much information hitherto unpublished. It is hoped that this information will be of use to urban planners and transit administrators. The questionnaire results also provide a clue as to the profile and attitudes of management in this important industry.

Analysis and Recommendations

The conclusions and recommendations of this study will, hopefully, be of interest to urban planners, public administrators, other groups interested in urban economic health (such as businessmen and the press) and executives of the transit industry. The first three groups, vitally concerned with fiscal and urban land use problems, should be interested in recommendations which might aid in insuring a better urban mass transit system, and consequently better urban transportation.

But perhaps the recommendations will be of greatest value to the existing and future administrators of urban mass transit companies. For their ability to attract riders, capital aid, and managerial talent to their industry may well determine the character and vitality of the transit industry and the cities it serves.

CHAPTER 2

The Mass Transportation Industry:
Past and Present

A Short History of Urban Mass Transit

The mass transportation industry, as defined by the American Transit Association, ". . . comprises all organized local passenger transportation agencies except taxicabs, suburban railroads, sight-seeing buses and school buses."[1] It thus includes urban and suburban companies providing bus, trolley bus, street railway, and rapid transit service.

The industry can trace its origins, in this country, back to 1827 when Abraham Brower commissioned the coach-making firm of Wade & Leverich to build a vehicle with a seating capacity of twelve. He operated his horse-drawn "Accommodation" up and down Broadway in New York City, charging a flat fare of "one shilling a head" regardless of the distance traveled.[2]

As the standard of living of the nation improved, and people found that they could afford to pay the price of transportation in order to secure better residential locations or travel to more

[1] American Transit Association, *Transit Fact Book: 1963 Edition* (New York: American Transit Association, 1963), p. i. Statistics pertaining to the urban mass transit industry, unless otherwise noted, have been taken from this source.

[2] John Anderson Miller, *Fares Please* (New York: Dover, 1960), p. 1.

distant jobs, the primitive horsecar lines began to thrive.[3] More entrepreneurs entered the field, and cities soon began to recognize that excessive competition was wasteful. In return for exclusive franchises to operate over certain routes, the early street railway companies had to submit to regulation over policies such as fares and equipment. Thus, early in its history, mass transportation became an industry serving two masters: private enterprise supplying the capital and expecting adequate returns on this capital; and the public interest, as vested in the municipal government.[4]

Between 1827 and 1888 many attempts were made to replace the horse as the method of motive power, for both humanitarian and economic reasons. Cable lines prospered in some cities, but were inflexible and costly. Steam "dummies" were also tried, and even compressed air was suggested as a propellant. But the technological breakthrough which enabled the industry to enter its greatest period of expansion was the adaptation of the electric motor to the horse car. On February 2, 1888, Frank Sprague opened his first car line in Richmond, and from then until the perfection of the motor bus in the 1930's, the urban mass transit industry was to be identified with the trolley car.

During the first quarter of the 20th century, traffic on the street railways rose consistently. The growing urban population moved out from the centers of the cities along new trolley routes. The downtown department store appeared in the central business districts (CBD), as the trolleys enabled large numbers of people to shop conveniently in central locations.[5]

[3] This brief history has been compiled from sources including: J. A. Miller; Frank Rowsome, Jr., *Trolley Car Treasury* (New York: McGraw-Hill, 1956); and Robert Futterman, *The Future of Our Cities* (Garden City: Doubleday, 1961), pp. 48–67. For a complete bibliography of the street railway industry's development, see Foster M. Palmer, "The Literature of the Street Railway," *Harvard Library Bulletin*, XII (Winter 1958), pp. 117–138.

[4] For a complete concise history of franchises and public regulation see Thomas Conway, "Franchises and Public Regulation," *Principles of Urban Transportation*, ed. Frank H. Mossman (Cleveland: Western Reserve University, 1951), pp. 21–32.

[5] George Sternlieb, *The Future of the Downtown Department Store* (Cambridge: Joint Center for Urban Studies of the Massachusetts Institute of Technology and Harvard University, 1962), p. 6. [Hereafter cited as Sternlieb.]

As the streets became congested with streetcars and horses and wagons, elevated and subway lines were constructed in New York City, Chicago, Philadelphia, and Boston. Every major city talked in terms of the new "rapid transit," although a major study made by the Bureau of the Census in 1902 warned:

> The chief difficulty which stands in the way of a rapid development of subway systems . . . is the heavy cost of construction . . . In New York . . . the present subway and tracks, exclusive of power houses and equipment, and of damages to abutting property, will cost . . . $1,750,000 per mile. . . . From the standpoint of profits . . . both elevated and subway railways intended for fast traffic are confronted by the facts that most of their passengers ride long distances, that a majority must be carried to a single business center; and that a very large proportion of the traffic is during the rush hours. As population, aided by the facilities offered, extends farther from the center of the city, these peculiarities will become more marked. Nevertheless, there is every reason to believe that, either through private or public enterprise, additional subways will gradually be constructed in New York and other cities.[6]

The warnings were justified, for the problems of rapid transit (high cost, long rides per passenger at low fares, concentrated destinations in the CBD, and peaking of traffic, intensified by the shifting of population to the suburbs) are as evident today, contributing to the "urban transportation problem."

But in the early 1900's all was optimistic. Capitalists made fortunes as the industry grew.[7] Young men saw urban mass transit as both a growing, yet stable, industry. In common with the railroads, many graduating mechanical, civil, and electrical engineering students joined street railway companies expecting a lucrative and fulfilling career.

This optimism seemed justified by the traffic. In 1905 local urban mass transit carried 5 billion passengers.[8] By 1926 and

[6] U.S. Bureau of the Census, *Special Reports—Street and Electric Railways 1902* (1905), p. 38.

[7] One very readable history of entrepreneurial activity during this period is Sidney I. Roberts, "Portrait of a Robber Baron: Charles T. Yerkes," *Business History Review*, XXXV (Autumn 1961), pp. 344–371.

[8] For statistics of the industry's growth and decline see American Transit Association Fact Books, Smith & Associates, p. 354, and Owen, p. 282.

1927 this figure had climbed to 17.2 billion annual passengers. Although the automobile had begun to appear on the streets, it was dismissed as a rich man's toy until the end of the First World War when the horseless carriages began to innundate the streets.

By 1933 the combined effects of the depression and the growing importance of the automobile slashed annual transit patronage to 11.3 billion riders. With the decline in patronage went the industry's hopes for modernization. During the 1930's new equipment was for the most part out of the question, and the antiquated "Toonerville Trolley" became the symbol of the financial plight of the industry. Traction stocks, once considered a necessary part of "widows' portfolios," became worthless as companies fell into bankruptcy.

The trend toward public ownership, originally stimulated by public claims of poor private management, accelerated.[9] The early large municipal properties—San Francisco (1912), Seattle (1919), and Detroit (1922)—were joined by New York City (1932, 1940) and Cleveland (1942).

The Second World War, however, suddenly reversed the downward trends as austerity curbed the automobile. Over 23 billion passengers rode during the year 1946 (before the pent-up demand for automobiles could be filled) and ridership per capita soared from 1933's 160 to 312 (1945). Ironically, this flood of traffic weakened some systems, for the low rates of fare were often insufficient to permit extensive modernization of the street railway lines. In other instances, wartime production restrictions prevented deliveries of new buses or the President's Conference Committee (PCC) streamlined streetcars to systems which could afford new equipment.

[9] Public ownership took one of three major forms: (1) Municipal, (2) Transit Authority, or (3) Transit District. For detailed descriptions of each form, including method of financing and appointment of the executive board, see: Norman Kennedy and Wolfgang S. Homburger, *The Organization of Metropolitan Transit Agencies* (Berkeley: University of California Institute of Transportation and Traffic Engineering, 1961). [Hereafter cited as Kennedy and Homburger, *Organization of Metropolitan Transit Agencies.*] Owen, pp. 191–217. City of Philadelphia, Mayor's Transit Study Task Force. *The Public Transit Authority—A Study of Five Cities* (Philadelphia: By the City, 1963).

Following the peak year 1946 a long-term secular decline in traffic began. Riding plummeted until rides per capita in 1953 were less than the depression year 1933. Again, declining patronage and financial distress initiated public ownership. Chicago (1947) and Boston (1947) joined the list of public properties as transit authorities, rather than municipal operations. New York City changed its form of public ownership from municipal to authority, and acquired several local bus companies during 1947 and 1948.

Another trend during the postwar period was the transition from private to public enterprise of financially prosperous systems. Several of these companies had been managed by National City Lines, Inc., a holding company which operated many properties in small cities and held controlling interest in major companies located in Los Angeles and Oakland, California, Baltimore, Maryland, St. Louis, Missouri, and Philadelphia, Pennsylvania.

During the 1940's City Lines followed a consistent policy of replacing streetcars with buses, instituting reforms in scheduling and cost control, upgrading maintenance facilities, and instituting new services such as express buses. However, its willingness to "take a strike," plus its petitions for fare increases, service cuts, and tax relief to preserve an adequate return on investment kept the City Lines' properties in a more or less continual state of battle with local public officials. By early 1964 the City Lines' holdings in St. Louis, Los Angeles, and Oakland had been absorbed by transit authorities and districts, and legislation had been passed to permit public acquisition of the remaining large properties in Philadelphia and Baltimore.[10] Also in 1964 the privately owned Pittsburgh Railways was taken over by the Allegheny County Port Authority, leaving Washington's D.C. Transit System as the only major transit company not imminently in danger of being purchased by public agencies.[11]

---

[10] The companies, date purchased, form of public ownership, and method of public purchase were as follows: St. Louis (1963, Authority, revenue bonds), Oakland (1960, District, taxes and bonds), and Los Angeles (1958, Authority, revenue bonds).

[11] *Passenger Transport,* March 6, 1964, p. 1.

In addition to forms of ownership, there were other notable changes affecting the industry during the postwar period. Perhaps the most dramatic, comparable to the dieselization of the railroads, was the replacement of the streetcar and the trolley coach by the diesel motor bus. In 1945 the industry gross investment in street railway plant and equipment totaled $1,570 million; motor buses, $566 million. By 1962 the street railway investment had been reduced to $229 million, whereas motor bus investment had climbed to $854 million. No new streetcars were purchased by the industry after 1952, and the total number of streetcars owned declined from 26,160 in 1945, to 2,219 in 1962. In comparison, motor coach ownership rose from 49,670 in 1945 to 57,660 in 1951, and in response to the decline in traffic and increased seating capacity in a coach, dropped to 48,800 by 1962.

The author is convinced that the abandonment of streetcars prevented financial collapse of the industry. Almost overnight, an industry with high fixed costs of maintenance of way, generation of power, and, in some cases, engineering and construction of rolling stock, found itself buying standardized products from a limited group of manufacturers, as well as relieved of the problem of maintenance of right of way. The motor bus brought other significant savings. In many cities, two-man streetcars were replaced with one-man buses. Routes were no longer tied to the inflexibility of the steel rail, and could follow the population growth into suburbia. Energies once devoted to keeping the "steel pipeline" filled with streetcars were turned to exploiting the flexibility of the bus in express service.

Properties which had formerly maintained buses, trolley coaches, and streetcars could standardize and reduce their parts inventories. Buses were free to "deadhead" to garages unrestricted by trolley overhead. Thus, many companies badly in need of new maintenance facilities were able to close down unneeded depots, sell excess real estate, and construct one large modern depot to service most, if not all, of the system. These large depots, in turn, resulted in consolidated rosters and more efficient use of manpower.

Buses brought problems, too. Because a bus could not carry as many passengers as a streetcar, labor costs on heavy routes sometimes increased, because more vehicles were dispatched to handle peak loads. In a few cities streetcar routes which were partially located on private rights of way were replaced by buses, which then had to fight street congestion. In other instances, e.g., Cleveland and Detroit, new PCC streamlined streetcars were sold at a loss as the system converted. But, more often than not, buses replaced old trolley cars, worn out from the heavy wartime service.

Unfortunately, the reduction in expenses from bus substitution was more than offset by rising labor costs and declining traffic. Between 1945 and 1962 the industry's annual revenue increased from $1.38 billion to only $1.4 billion (even though revenue per passenger almost tripled); annual patronage declined 62%; payroll costs increased $246 million (despite a cut in the workforce of 92,900); net operating income fell from $148.7 to $20.2 million; and return on investment dropped from 3.5% to almost 0.5%.

Thus, as transit entered the 1960's, the industry had come the full cycle, from technological development and growth under private enterprise, through maturity and some degree of complacency when first threatened by the automobile, to a secular declining demand for its product and financial uncertainty.

The Urban Mass Transit Industry Today

Measures of Size and Scale

In 1962 the 1,205 operating companies reporting financial and statistical data to the American Transit Association (representing more than 85% of the transit industry) took in operating revenue of $1,403 million, while carrying 8,695 million total (including transfer) passengers and 7,122 million revenue passengers. The industry paid $878.1 million in wages to its 149,100 employees and had a gross investment of $4,002 million ($2,813 million of which represented subway and elevated plant and equipment).

A relatively small number of companies accounts for the majority of industry activity. For example, the twelve companies serving the twelve largest cities of the United States[12] represent only 1% of the total number of companies in the industry, yet in 1961 accounted for 51.9% of the total transit revenue passengers (surface plus rapid transit), 99.6% of the total industry rapid transit riders, 52.2% of the operating revenue, and 61.0% of the gross investment. Because of the importance of scale in the industry, the statistical analysis in this study was arbitrarily confined to this sample of companies. Table 2.1 indicates the names of these companies, their identifying initials, and the cities in which they were located.

The names of the companies and cities will frequently be used interchangeably in the remainder of this study. It should be noted that the New York City Transit Authority (NYCTA) dominates the sample and the industry. In 1961 NYCTA handled 81% of the total industry rapid transit riders and 25% of the total transit revenue passengers (surface plus rapid transit).[13] Its gross investment, largely representing its rapid transit plant and equipment, was 44% of the total industry gross investment. No other domestic city approaches the scope of the NYCTA in terms of traffic or investment. For example, the annual traffic (surface plus rapid transit) of the Chicago Transit Authority (CTA), the second largest system in the nation, is less than 30% of that of the NYCTA. In view of the unique status of the NYCTA and the transportation problems of the New York metropolitan area, the author has deliberately excluded New

[12] The author has ranked the cities by Standard Metropolitan Statistical Area rather than by central city population (used by the American Transit Association) to acknowledge the importance of the suburban element in the urban transportation picture. For the definitions of SMSA and central city population see U.S. Bureau of the Census, *U.S. Census of Population; 1960 Number of Inhabitants United States Summary*, Final Report PC (1)–1A (1961), pp. ix-xxvii. [Hereafter cited as *1960 Census*.]

[13] New York City's central business district was primarily served by the New York City Transit Authority, Surface Transit Company, and Fifth Avenue Coach Lines until 1962, when the city through a subsidiary of the Transit Authority confiscated the Fifth Avenue and Surface Lines properties. Throughout this study, statistics referring to the sample company in New York City include only the New York City Transit Authority and exclude its Fifth Avenue—Surface Lines subsidiary as well as other large independent transit operations such as the Triboro Coach Corp.

Table 2.1

Sample of Major Transit Companies Used in This Study

Name of City	Name of Company	Initials
New York City	New York City Transit Authority	NYCTA
Los Angeles	Los Angeles Metropolitan Transit Authority*	LAMTA
Chicago	Chicago Transit Authority	CTA
Philadelphia	Philadelphia Transportation Company†	PTC
Detroit	Department of Street Railways	DSR
San Francisco	Municipal Railway of San Francisco	MRSF
Boston	Metropolitan Transit Authority‡	MTA
Pittsburgh	Pittsburgh Railways†	PRWYS
St. Louis	St. Louis Public Service Company†	STLPS
Washington, D.C.	D.C. Transit System†	DCTS
Cleveland	Cleveland Transit System	CTS
Baltimore	Baltimore Transit Company†	BTC

* On August 22, 1964, the Southern California Rapid Transit District was established to serve the greater Los Angeles metropolitan area. It is anticipated that the District will absorb the Los Angeles Metropolitan Transit Authority.

† Indicates private operation as of the year 1962, when the author made his field trips and statistical analyses. The St. Louis Public Service Company was purchased by the Bi-State Transit Authority in 1963. The Pittsburgh Railways was acquired by powers of condemnation of the Allegheny County Port Authority in 1964.

‡ Absorbed in 1964 by the Massachusetts Bay Transportation Authority (MBTA). See Chapter 4 for details.

York from his field case studies, for to generalize from New York's experience would probably be both unrealistic and misleading.[14]

Measures of Patronage, Revenue, and Profits of Large Urban Mass Transit Companies

In order to give the reader a better indication of the economic status of the dominant transit companies in the industry, this

[14] See Meyer et. al., p. vii. Though differing greatly from this author in their conclusions on rapid transit, these authors agree that New York City's transit problem is unique in the United States.

section of the chapter will focus briefly on the traffic and financial data of the twelve sample companies.

Patronage: Table 2.2 indicates the number of revenue passengers (broken down into rapid transit and surface) carried by the sample companies and the total industry for selected years between 1940 and 1962. Table 2.3 converts these aggregate data into percentage changes, using the year 1960 as the base.

The most apparent fact is the diversity within a general pattern of secular decline. Each of the companies has seen its traffic plummet between 1945 and 1962. It is clear that the strongest performances during the period 1955–1962 were made by New York (both surface and rapid transit), Chicago (rapid transit only), Philadelphia (rapid transit), Cleveland, (rapid transit), Boston (rapid transit),[15] San Francisco, and Washington. St. Louis, Detroit, Los Angeles, and Pittsburgh (none of which possessed rapid transit) had relatively poorer patronage.

Thus, the publicly operated systems, particularly those with rapid transit, tended to have the best patronage trends during the postwar period. Washington, D.C., the only private company not operating rapid transit to make a strong showing, undoubtedly was aided by the fact that the District of Columbia was both third in the nation in metropolitan growth (1940–1960) as well as fourth in downtown daytime population (behind New York City, Chicago, and Philadelphia).[16]

Profitability: A common measure of operating efficiency in the transportation industry is the operating ratio (operating expense/operating revenue). However, because of extremely different depreciation practices and tax liabilities within the mass transit industry, tabulations of operating ratios by the author have been made excluding depreciation, taxes, interest, other income, and extraordinary charges.

[15] Boston's passenger statistics are not broken down into rapid transit and surface traffic. The 1962 passenger estimate and the assumption that the MTA's rapid transit traffic is holding up better than its surface traffic are contained in reports of the Massachusetts Mass Transportation Commission.

[16] U.S. National Capital Transportation Agency, *Recommendations for Transportation in the National Capital Region* (1962), pp. 7–8. [Hereafter cited as *1962 Capital Region Transportation Plan.*]

Table 2.2

Transit Revenue Passengers in Sample Cities: Selected Years, 1940–1962

(In millions)

Company	1940	1945	1950	1955	1958	1959	1960	1961	1962
New York City									
Rapid Transit	1,844	1,953	1,660	1,362	1,323	1,329	1,349	1,360	1,384
Surface	545	660	621	415	414	421	433	436	452
Los Angeles	232	430	315	194	182	184	167	153	148
Chicago									
Rapid Transit	124	157	111	113	107	113	113	110	114
Surface	730	920	723	511	426	433	422	395	391
Philadelphia									
Rapid Transit	94	140	113	84	76	73	75	77	73
Surface	329	563	439	302	266	261	253	240	237
Detroit	263	466	324	210	150	141	130	118	115
San Francisco	174	252	183	144	140	141	141	141	141
Boston	294	420	308	224	205	201	199	NA	180
Pittsburgh	159	280	221	111	85	80	76	71	64
St. Louis	155	335	216	135	99	98	92	83	73
Washington*	250	532	352	169	176	176	176	175	170
Cleveland									
Rapid Transit*		Not	Available	8.1	15.5	17.8	18.3	17.8	17.3
Surface									
Baltimore	143	264	195	132	109	101	99	95	94
Total United States	10,504	18,982	13,845	9,189	7,778	7,650	7,521	7,242	7,122

SOURCE: American Transit Association.

* Total, not revenue, passengers.

Table 2.3

Percentage Change in Transit Revenue Passengers in Sample Cities: Selected Years, 1940–1962 (1960 = 100)

Company	1940	1945	1950	1955	1958	1959	1960	1961	1962
New York City									
Rapid Transit	136.7	144.8	123.1	101.0	98.1	98.5	100.0	100.8	102.6
Surface	125.9	152.4	143.4	95.8	95.6	97.2	100.0	100.7	104.4
Los Angeles	138.9	257.5	188.6	116.2	109.0	110.2	100.0	91.6	88.6
Chicago									
Rapid Transit	109.7	138.9	98.2	100.0	94.7	100.0	100.0	97.3	100.9
Surface	173.0	218.0	171.3	121.1	100.9	102.6	100.0	93.6	92.7
Philadelphia									
Rapid Transit	125.3	186.7	150.7	112.0	101.3	97.3	100.0	102.7	97.3
Surface	130.0	222.5	173.5	119.4	105.1	103.2	100.0	94.9	93.7
Detroit	202.3	358.5	249.2	161.5	115.4	108.5	100.0	90.8	88.5
San Francisco	123.4	178.7	129.8	102.1	99.3	100.0	100.0	100.0	100.0
Boston	147.7	211.1	154.8	112.6	103.0	101.0	100.0	NA	90.5
Pittsburgh	209.2	368.4	290.8	146.1	111.8	105.3	100.0	93.4	84.2
St. Louis	168.5	364.1	234.8	146.7	107.6	106.5	100.0	90.2	79.3
Washington, D.C.	142.0	302.3	200.0	96.0	100.0	100.0	100.0	99.4	96.6
Cleveland									
Rapid Transit	Not	Avai	lable	44.3	84.7	97.3	100.0	97.3	94.5
Surface									
Baltimore	144.4	266.7	197.0	133.3	110.1	102.0	100.0	96.0	94.9
Total United States	139.7	252.4	184.1	122.2	103.4	101.7	100.0	96.3	94.7

Source: Table 2.2.

Table 2.4 shows that some companies operating rapid transit, e.g., New York City, Chicago, and Boston, tended to have high operating ratios, yet Philadelphia and Cleveland did not. Most of the cities which had been successful in retaining traffic had high operating ratios, e.g., New York, Chicago, San Francisco, Boston, and Washington. It is interesting to note that the three companies with the lowest operating ratios, excluding depreciation and taxes (Baltimore, Philadelphia, and St. Louis), were each privately owned and managed by National City Lines.

It can definitely be concluded that in 1961 the public companies had a more unfavorable operating performance than the private firms. The average public operating ratio, excluding depreciation and taxes, was 97.0; whereas the private was 79.8. Inasmuch as the numerator of the operating ratio depends upon fares and patronage, and the denominator is determined by operating expenses, it is extremely difficult to generalize as to the relative performance of public and private companies. Important factors include price policies, political pressures, and labor pressures. Each will be discussed briefly during the remainder of this study. In some cases, public companies have been forced to acquire unprofitable small bus companies along with the major private company serving an urban area. Or the poor financial performance may reflect the fact that factors beyond the control of transit managements in certain cities made transit operations inherently unprofitable either under private or, subsequently, public operation. It should be noted that this study has not attempted to consider in depth the question of the relative performance of public versus private companies. To have done so would have required resources beyond those available to the author.

The twelve companies had one ominous statistic in common, the inability to generate profits sufficient to permit internal, or attract external, financing for major capital investment projects. In 1961 the impact of depreciation, fixed charges, and taxes reduced the operating profit of $48.7 million to a net loss of $16.5 million (Table 2.4). Even with depreciation charges added back, the cash flow of these twelve companies (61% of the industry's gross investment) was only $13.2 million. Again, the private companies displayed better financial performance with a

Table 2.4

Financial Analysis of Sample Transit Companies: 1961
(In millions)

Public Companies	(a) Operating Revenue	(b) Operating Expense[1]	Ratio (b)/(a)	(c) Net Income	(d) Depreciation[2]	(e) Cash Flow
New York	$281.3	$280.1	99.6	$ 2.1[3]	—	$ 2.1[3]
Los Angeles	44.9	38.1[4]	84.9	1.1	$ 4.0	5.1
Chicago	128.7	112.6	87.5	3.7[5]	10.3[6]	14.0
Detroit	30.8	25.7	83.4	1.5	2.4	3.9
San Francisco	19.8	24.7	124.7	(6.0)	1.0	(5.0)
Boston	36.7	48.3	131.6	(20.1)	1.2	(18.9)
Cleveland	26.8	22.4	83.6	.97	1.9	2.8
Totals	$569.0	$551.9	97.0	$(16.8)	$20.8	$ 4.0
Private Companies						
Philadelphia	65.9	50.5	76.6	(1.5)[8]	4.1	2.6
Pittsburgh	19.1	17.2	90.1	(.5)	1.4	.9
St. Louis	20.1	15.5	77.1	.7	1.2	1.9
Washington	29.7	25.1[9]	84.5	.9	1.1[10]	2.0
Baltimore	21.7	16.6	76.5	.7	1.1	1.8
Totals	$156.5	$124.9	79.8	$ .3	$ 8.9	$ 9.2
Grand Totals	$725.5[11]	$676.8		$(16.5)	$29.7	$13.2

[1] Operating expenses excluding depreciation, fixed charges, extraordinary expenses, miscellaneous deductions, and taxes.

[2] Depreciation and other noncash charges added back.

[3] Revenues include $23 million in payments by city for school subsidy, power, and police protection. City pays interest and debt retirement which in 1961 amounted to $96.2 million, and if included in columns (d) and (e) would have produced substantial deficits.

[4] Slightly overstated because expenses include state and local sales taxes.

[5] Net income insufficient to cover sinking funds and prior depreciation by $843,000.

[6] Net of $10.4 million depreciation and $0.1 million amortization credit of bond discount.

[7] Under CTS accounting practice this net was immediately reduced to about $94,000 because of redemption of debt.

[8] Includes extraordinary charges of $2.6 million.

[9] Does not include $1 million track removal expense. This cost is reflected in net income.

[10] Net of $2.1 million depreciation and $1 million amortization credit arising from excess of net original cost of property recorded by predecessor over cost of present owner.

[11] 52.2% of industry total of $1,389.7 million.

Sources: *Moody's Transportation and Government Manuals,* Annual Reports, and American Transit Association, *1962 Fact Book.*

cash flow of $9.2 million. Yet the industry's needs for capital are enormous. One estimate says that $9.8 billion will be needed between 1962 and 1971 for modernization and expansion.[17]

The Demand for Urban Mass Transportation

As discussed in Chapter 1, the transit industry has been the subject of a great many studies during the past decade. The major findings of these surveys with respect to the consumer demand for mass transit will be summarized briefly below.

Purpose of the Trip

Urban mass transit in our largest cities specializes in the home-to-work trip.[18] In particular, rapid transit trips are work oriented. In both Chicago and Philadelphia approximately 70% of the rapid transit but only 47% of the surface transit riders having their home as a trip origin were traveling to work.[19]

The mass transit industry has been relatively less successful in attracting persons making shopping and recreational trips. In our largest cities 85% or more of such trips are made typically by automobile.[20]

On the other hand, the home-to-school trip in many cities is the only segment of the transit business displaying an increase in traffic. Approximately 15% of the surface mass transit riders

[17] U.S. Congress, Senate, Committee on Banking and Currency, *Hearings, Urban Mass Transportation,* 87th Cong., 2d Sess. (1962), p. 78. [Hereafter cited as *Senate, Urban Mass Transit 1962.*] For another recent forecast see Paul S. Jones and John L. Crain, "The $10 Billion Transit Market If . . ," *Metropolitan Transportation,* LX (January 1964), pp. 16–18. They estimated that $10 billion will have to be invested in rail rapid transit by 1985 to serve logically the increasing population of our cities.

[18] For example, the 1960 U.S. Census for the first time included questions on the mode of transportation used to reach work. For an analysis of the Census findings, see Henry J. Schmandt and G. Ross Stephens, "Public Transportation and the Worker," *Traffic Quarterly,* XVII (October 1963), pp. 573–583.

[19] *Chicago Area Transportation Study* (Chicago: Chicago Area Transportation Study, 1959–1962), I, p. 72, and Penn-Jersey Transportation Study, *P-J News* (August-September 1962), p. 4.

[20] Smith & Associates, p. 89.

in Chicago and Philadelphia were making school trips. In Pittsburgh the percentage of school-oriented mass transit riders was 33%.[21] School traffic unfortunately is a mixed blessing. Fares are usually low and the costs of service (vandalism included) are high, for school traffic intensifies the morning peak-load problem.

The importance of school trips points up the fact that many transit riders do not have access to an automobile for a given trip. It has been found in Chicago that 73% of the bus and 50% of the rapid transit riders could not have made the trip surveyed by auto.[22] In Pittsburgh this percentage rose to 85%.[23] Of course, a portion of this group is the aforementioned school trips, but the residual indicates that many persons because of income or inability cannot use an automobile for urban trips.

Timing of Mass Transit Trips

In view of the importance of work and school trips, it is not surprising that transit patronage tends to cluster during the hours of 7:00–9:00 a.m. and 4:00–6:00 p.m. This tendency has blessed and cursed transit from its earliest days. In 1902 the Metropolitan Street Railway (of New York City) estimated that 35% of its total traffic was carried during the peak hours.[24] In those days, when off-peak traffic was relatively high, this rush-hour traffic was accommodated simply through the device of overloading the cars normally on the routes. Charles T. Yerkes, builder and looter of the Chicago Street Railways, replied to stockholders who complained about crowded rush hour cars, "It is the people who hang on to the straps who pay you your big dividends."[25]

By the 1960's the decline of the shopping and social-recreation trips intensified the peak-load problem, not so much by raising the peaks, but by lowering the troughs. Peak-hour loads in major

---

[21] *Pittsburgh Area Transportation Study* (Pittsburgh: Pittsburgh Area Transportation Study, 1961–1963), I, p. 82. The figures for Chicago and Philadelphia are found on the pages cited in footnote 19.

[22] *Chicago Area Transportation Study*, I, p. 72.

[23] *Pittsburgh Area Transportation Study*, I, p. 82.

[24] U.S. Census, *Street and Electric Railways*, 1902, p. 33.

[25] Roberts, "Portrait of a Robber Baron," p. 352.

cities now represent as much as 40% of the surface passengers and 65% of the daily rapid transit riders.[26] Today the difference between the peaks and troughs is too great to permit the vehicles used in base service alone to handle the peak loads, and transit companies must operate two to three times the number of base vehicles in the peak hours.

Trip Destinations

The typical patron of urban mass transit not only is going to or from work during the rush hours, but also is destined for the central area of the city. Again, this tendency is more accentuated in rapid transit than bus travel. Rapid transit lines can achieve the densities of volume necessary to support the investment in plant and equipment only by delivering riders to a common destination. This destination, except for special occurrences, is the downtown area of the city. In turn, the percentage of all persons entering the central business district (transit + automobile) handled by transit is significant. In recent years this percentage in the largest cities has ranged from 78% (New York City) to 25% (Los Angeles).[27]

Since urban mass transit in our largest cities tends to concentrate on carrying persons to workplaces located in the central business district during peak periods of the day, it stands to reason that transit's best showing on a "share of the market basis" will be the percentage of persons entering or leaving the central business district during peak hours.

In actuality, mass transit does display impressive statistics of this kind. In 1961 the Chicago Transit Authority carried 50% of the peak rush-hour traffic, 111,000 persons, from the central district.[28] In 1960 New York City's subway system alone handled

[26] Smith & Associates, pp. 122–126; *Doyle Report*, pp. 598–600; Meyer et al., pp. 52–56; and *Collapse of Commuter Service*, pp. 2, 11.

[27] The percentages for other major cities include Chicago 59%, Philadelphia 59%, Boston 58%, Cleveland 42%, San Francisco 49%, Baltimore 31%, and St. Louis 28%. See Smith & Associates, p. 100; City of Cleveland, *1961 Cordon Count* (Cleveland: City of Cleveland, 1961); and Penn-Jersey Transportation Study, *P-J News* (August–September 1962), p. 3.

[28] Chicago Transit Authority, *Trend of Passenger Traffic Leaving the Central District During the Peak Evening Hour by Mode of Transportation* (Chicago: CTA, 1962). It should be noted that in addition to those peak-hour

almost 600,000 riders, about 70% of all persons entering and leaving the CBD during the peak hour.[29] In other large cities mass transit typically carries about 30% to 70% of the peak-hour load.[30]

In view of the above statistics, it can reasonably be concluded that any justification for extensive urban mass transit systems in our largest cities rests on two arguments: to carry those who cannot drive a car, and/or to handle as a part of a balanced transportation network embodying the private auto and high capacity vehicles, the peak-hour requirements to and from the central business district. Many believe that this latter function may well determine the fate of our largest urban areas. This point of view, and its critics, will be treated more fully in the following chapter.

The Mass Transit Company: A Functional Description

Having reviewed the basic statistical characteristics of the industry and the demand for its service, it is appropriate to complete this overview of the industry by focusing attention on the formal tasks and organization of the typical transit company.

In many respects a transit company is no different from any manufacturing enterprise. It utilizes a combination of fixed assets and manpower to produce a product, and attempts to sell that product so as to cover manufacturing and overhead costs and produce a profit sufficient for modernization of the system. A private transit company's profit, hopefully, will also cover dividends to its stockholders.

The critical difference between a transit and a manufacturing company is that the product produced is an elusive one. It can be produced at will, but never stored, and it is known under various names: car miles, bus miles, or seat miles, depending on

---

passengers carried by CTA, the commuter railroads haul almost 30% of the peak travel. Similar statistics are evident in New York City, where approximately 10% of the peak traffic is handled by commuter railroads.

[29] Regional Plan Association, *Hub Bound Travel in the Tri-State Metropolitan Region* (New York: Regional Plan Association, 1961).

[30] *Doyle Report*, p. 599.

the technological configuration of the company and its standards of comfort. (For example, drawing from another segment of the transportation industry, airlines report capacity in terms of seat miles, as standees are not permitted.) Inasmuch as the demand for mass transit is confined largely to a few hours per week, and transit's product cannot be produced in advance and stored, it is clear that profitable operation is not easy.

To produce and sell its service, most transit companies are organized according to the following functional areas: transportation (often, though not always, including scheduling), maintenance, purchasing and stores, engineering, personnel, comptroller-treasurer, public relations, legal, and planning. Figures 2.1 and 2.2 show how two large companies have delegated authority and responsibility for performance of these functions. Each department will be discussed briefly below.

Transportation: The transportation (sometimes called operating) department represents 40% to 60% of the total operating expenses. It is administered by a general superintendent through superintendents, depot superintendents, and roving supervisors. These men are responsible for the day-to-day production plan by dispatching vehicles and drivers, checking to see if schedules are being adhered to, and administering "job picks." In some companies, transportation recruits and trains drivers. The group often contains a statistical section which develops data on labor and other operating costs per vehicle mile and vehicle hour.

Schedules: The schedule department produces the master and daily production plan. Its inputs are vehicle running times, passenger checks at peak-load points for each route, and management policy on loading standards. Either manually or with the aid of data processing equipment, this information is analyzed and a timetable is prepared for each route. The timetable is then converted into a list of "jobs" called "runs." Employees periodically bid for these runs by seniority. The production plan (schedule) determines future vehicle mileage (timetable) and pay hours (list of runs) and quite commonly determines about 65% of the total company operating costs, which vary with hours or mileage.

Figure 2.1

Partial Organization Chart
Chicago Transit Authority

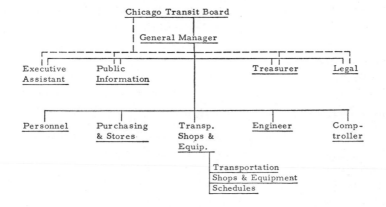

Figure 2.2

Partial Organization Chart
Cleveland Transit System

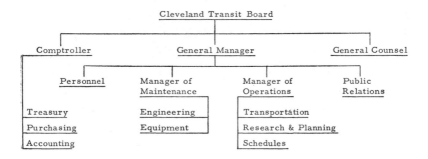

NOTE: Both of these charts show only a portion of the functions in a transit company. These major functions are discussed in the text.

Maintenance: This function represents 10% to 20% of total expenses, but will not be analyzed in this study.

Purchasing and Stores: This function will also not be treated in this study.

Engineering: The engineering department is particularly important in companies operating rapid transit or electric surface vehicles. It is responsible for ways and structures, specifications, and evaluating capital projects. The chief engineer's staff generally has the largest percentage of college graduates, and in some companies constitutes a major source of future management personnel.

Personnel: This function was handled historically by the transportation department. It performs normal personnel duties (recruiting, training, clerical) and aids in gathering data for labor negotiations. In some companies, the personnel department is also responsible for handling grievance proceedings.

Comptroller-Treasurer: In many companies this function is split between two officers. The combined function is responsible for accounting, auditing, cash management, revenue forecasts and financial planning, and sometimes the compilation of other cost data (e.g., labor). Most companies have introduced electric accounting or electronic data processing equipment for payroll and other tasks through this department.

Public Relations: This is a staff function responsible for relations with the press and public as well as promotion and advertising.

Legal: The legal staff is particularly important because of regulatory problems, claims, and, recently, legal arrangements surrounding federal aid. The general counsel also often handles much of the labor relations testimony before arbitration boards, etc.

Planning: Few companies have a separate planning department although planning and research are carried out in many departments (e.g., engineering, schedules, comptroller, transportation). But some companies have separate planning staffs. Sometimes this "staff" is one man, an executive assistant to the chief administrative officer.

Even this brief listing of the departments points to a major characteristic of the transit industry: the formal organization is production rather than marketing oriented, and functionally rather than product or project organized. There simply are no vice presidents—marketing, directors of commuter operations, supervisors of off-peak services, or even project managers (once the line is in operation) of new rapid transit lines. The organization chart reflects the fact that the overwhelming majority of the company's activities is devoted to the two production functions: transportation and maintenance.

This emphasis on production is not surprising when a closer look is taken at the production task. The job of dispatching and supervising over 1,000 vehicles (without radio) on the city streets, maintaining these vehicles, and compensating the men who drive them requires a staggering amount of detailed statistical data. Peak-load checks must be taken, running times checked, headways calculated, schedules and runs cut, jobs picked, maintenance records kept, daily cash receipts audited, and adjustments made constantly because of traffic conditions, school changes, variations in the weather, etc.

The major friction within this operating framework centers on the schedule department, which must balance the demands of labor and management and produce daily schedules. Labor constantly pleads for more runs and more running time, whereas management tries to minimize men and vehicle requirements within the limits of adequate service.

There are other problem areas. Within the transportation department there may be serious conflicts between supervisors and drivers, stemming from the complexities of the labor agreement, plus the impossibility of direct supervision, at all times, during the work day.

In other situations, the engineering or public relations sections may press for revisions in routes, equipment, or fares which might make the administrative problems of the transportation department that much more difficult. Such conflicts are usually resolved by the chief administrative officer or an operating committee composed of the heads of the functional departments.

There are some variations on the general functional framework described above, and the case studies will point up some of these differences. But the key observation remains: a transit company is organized primarily to produce, not sell, its product.

Summary

This chapter has been necessarily brief. Following a short history of the industry (characterized by declining traffic, a technological shift from streetcars to buses, and the transition from private to public ownership), the text turned to a description and analysis of the industry's present position.

The analysis of a sample of transit companies in our largest cities revealed common patterns of patronage (rush-hour CBD work, necessity, and school trips) as well as financial distress. Finally, consideration of the role of a transit company, and its functional organization, suggested that the organization chart reflects the importance and the difficulty of fulfilling the day-to-day production plan, moving thousands of persons safely within the urban area.

This organizational, financial, and patronage pattern has resulted from the interaction of a complex network of pressures which must be clearly understood before management strategy is studied in depth.

CHAPTER 3

The Environment of Strategy

A Model for the Analysis of Transit Management Strategy

Decision making in the mass transportation industry does not take place in a vacuum. The administrator is continually confronted by a host of variables, both within and beyond his direct or indirect control. This complex network can be represented by a simple flow chart (Figure 3.1). Three kinds of paths link the variables shown.[1]

Indirect External Pressures

These forces are beyond the direct control of transit management, but they influence factors which have a direct bearing on the economic health of the industry. For example, government promotion of highways will directly affect consumer demand for mass transit, and ultimately the number of transit passengers carried during specific hours of the day. Or the government may enact legislation which makes it easier for private sources to supply the industry with capital. An important indirect pressure exists in the ability of the general public or special interest groups to cause changes in the government's policies of promotion, regulation, and pressure through voting and other elements of the governmental process.

[1] Not all possible pressures and strategies are shown (for example, maintenance is excluded), but only those which the author believes are particularly significant.

Figure 3.1

External Pressures and Mass Transit Strategies

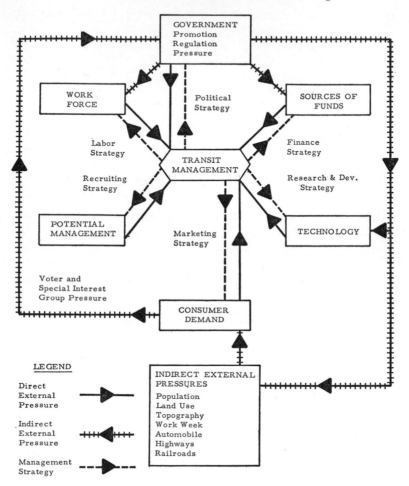

Direct External Pressures

The chart is self-explanatory. The principal factors directly affecting management's performance include: pressures from labor, attitudes of individuals who form a pool of potential future management, the attitudes of sources of capital, the developments in technology, activities of the government, and consumer demand for mass transit. It should be noted that the nature of consumer demand has been discussed in Chapter 2.

Management Strategy

Management strategy constitutes its response to each of the above direct external pressures. A strategy is defined as a set of policies keyed toward a desired objective. Thus, marketing strategy encompasses the mix of price, product planning, promotion, and market research policies. Likewise, political strategy consists of a set of policies, such as techniques of direct and indirect legislative access designed to meet the pressures of government promotion, regulation, and pressure.

Formal Organization and the Flow Chart

As discussed in Chapters 1 and 2, a major concern of this study is the pattern of formal organization in the transit industry. It is important, however, to understand that formal organization, as such, is not shown on the flow chart, for the chart represents strategic, not functional, decisions.

Indirect External Pressures

Importance of These Pressures

The remainder of this and the following chapter will be used to analyze each of the factors shown on the flow chart. This process will establish the importance of marketing strategy in the priority of management decision areas.

One of the more interesting findings of the author's transit executive questionnaire was that six of the nine respondents chose "declining demand for the service caused by factors *beyond* the control of management" as the industry's single most important problem (Question 2).

On the other hand, only one of eight respondents agreed with a statement from one transportation study which painted a bleak picture of the transit industry's future (Question 8). In fact, most of the executives felt that revenue passengers, passenger revenue, net operating income, and net income would remain within 10% of 1962 levels during the period 1962–1967 (Table 3.1).

Table 3.1

Questionnaire Responses:
Forecast of Transit Industry Activity

During 1962–1967 the Following Will	+10%	−10%	Remain Within 10%	Total Responses
Revenue passengers	—	4	5	9
Passenger revenue	1	1	7	9
Net operating income	1	2	6	9
Net income	1	2	6	9
Charter and special service revenue (e.g., tours)	5	1	3	9

SOURCE: Question 3.

In view of management's concern with factors beyond its control, the indirect external pressures on the transit industry will be discussed first.

Population

During the decade 1950–1960 the nation's population increased by 28 million, nearly as great as that during the two decades 1930–1950.[2] The bulk of this increase, 23.6 million, took place within standard metropolitan statistical areas (SMSA). Population within SMSA's increased 26.4%, whereas the rest of the country's population increased only 7.1%. Within these SMSA's, central city population increased 10.7%, but the population of that portion of the SMSA's outside central cities increased 48.6%. Indeed, 11 of the 12 sample cities experienced declines in central city population (as high as 13%), although in each case the SMSA population increased (Table 3.2).

These trends are expected to continue. One major study forecasts that the 1980 population of the United States will be 245 million, with 75% residing in urban areas.[3] By the year 2000, 85% of our population is expected to live in urban areas with

[2] U.S. Business and Defense Services Administration, Office of Marketing Service, *Changing Metropolitan Markets, 1950–1960* (1961), p. 4.

[3] According to census terminology, "urban areas" are the sum total of central city, urbanized fringes, and urban places outside of urbanized areas populations, e.g. all places in the United States possessing urban character-

Table 3.2

Population Statistics:
Sample Cities and United States Total, 1960 Census
(Population figures in thousands)

City	Central City Pop.	% Change 1950– 1960	SMSA Total	% Change 1950– 1960	Population Area Served by Major Transit Co.
New York	7,782	(1.4)%	10,695	11.9%	4,900
Los Angeles	2,823	27.1	6,743	54.4	7,111
Chicago	3,550	(1.9)	6,221	20.1	3,550
Philadelphia	2,003	(3.3)	4,343	18.3	2,736
Detroit	1,670	(9.7)	3,762	24.7	1,960
San Francisco	1,108	(4.5)	2,783	24.2	753
Boston	697	(13.0)	2,589	7.4	1,328
Pittsburgh	604	(10.7)	2,405	8.7	1,071
St. Louis	750	(12.5)	2,060	19.8	1,100
Washington	764	(4.8)	2,002	36.7	530
Cleveland	876	(4.2)	1,797	22.6	1,475
Baltimore	939	(1.1)	1,727	22.9	1,167
Total United States	58,004	10.7%	112,885	26.4%	—

SOURCES: U.S. Bureau of the Census, *U.S. Census of Population: 1960 Number of Inhabitants, United States Summary*. Final Report PC (1)–1A Table 33. American Transit Association, letter to the author.

107 million of these living in ten supermetropolises ranging in size from 5 to 23 million people.[4] Other studies predict similar patterns: relatively small growth within central cities, but major increases in SMSA's outside of central cities.[5]

The implications of this growth pattern on urban mass transit can be seen by comparing the American Transit Association's estimate of the "population of the area served by the major transit company" to the SMSA population in the sample cities. In

---

istics. Between 1950 and 1960 the percentage of the total domestic population residing in urban areas increased from 64% to 69.9%. The forecast for 1980 is in Smith & Associates, p. 10.

[4] Jerome Pickard, *The Metropolitanization of the United States*, quoted in *The Human Need for Rapid Transportation* (Mansfield: Ohio Brass, 1960), p. 1.

[5] *Doyle Report*, pp. 583–585, and Smith & Associates, pp. 9–14.

most cases, the "area served population" includes all of the central city, but only a small portion of the SMSA outside the central city. The reason is that transit best serves residential areas of high population density relatively close to the central business district. Both factors mean heavy loads with a minimum of vehicle miles and pay hours, and thus profitable operation. The transit industry feels that the low population densities of the suburbs cannot support full-scale transit service. On the other hand, it is clear that these major urban mass transit companies have failed to serve the areas of greatest urban growth during the past decade. This trend can only continue if population continues to decentralize and mass transit companies fail to extend their routes.

There have been significant demographic changes within this pattern of population growth which affect mass transit usage. Median family incomes increased 84% between 1949 and 1959, and the relative number of families with incomes below $3,000 fell from 46% to 21.4%.[6] Statistical correlations have shown that as income increases persons take more trips, and in turn make more of these trips by automobile.[7] Most of the increased trips, however, are nonwork oriented, the kind most difficult for transit to attract.

The second major change is the growing relative importance of persons under 18 years and over 65 in the total population.[8] The travel habits of the old and young are difficult to project. Vernon, in an extremely thought-provoking article, believes that older persons will move from the central city and probably not ride transit.[9] On the other hand, these two groups at the tails of

[6] Commonwealth of Massachusetts, Mass Transportation Commission, *The Boston Region,* prepared by Melvin R. Levin, (Boston: Mass Transportation Commission, 1963), p. 20.

[7] Smith & Associates, pp. 62, 79, and Walter Y. Oi and Paul Shuldiner, *An Analysis of Urban Travel Demands.*

[8] Hans H. Landsberg, Leonard L. Fischman, and Joseph L. Fisher, *Resources in America's Future, Patterns of Requirements and Availabilities, 1960–2000* (Baltimore: Johns Hopkins Press for Resources for the Future Inc., 1963), pp. 518–519. [Hereafter cited as Landsberg et al.] This massive study serves as a basic reference on existing and future levels of our nation's resources.

[9] Raymond Vernon, "The Economics and Finances of the Large Metropolis," *Daedelus* XC (Winter, 1961), p. 32.

the population distribution are least likely to have access to an automobile for a given trip. As this pool of "necessity riders" grows, perhaps transit can increase its patronage.

Changes in Land Use

A traveler arriving by airplane at any of our largest cities immediately perceives the changes in land use that the population trends imply. What was farm land ten years ago now supports residential, industrial, and commercial activity.

The rush to the suburbs has been stimulated by a variety of factors: high taxes (but poor services such as education), the desire to avoid racial integration, the attractiveness of FHA "no down payment" financing, the urge to enjoy the luxuries of a back yard and front lawn, space for efficient one-story plants and warehouses, and the mobility of the automobile and motor truck.

Some planners and economists have applauded this trend by noting that the mobility of industry has created a homogeneity of land use in the suburbs. They believe that persons will thus be able to live close to their places of employment, yet enjoy the advantages of suburban life.

On the other hand, the new exurbanites have left behind them residential and industrial blight. Blight is costly. It generally houses the elderly, the impoverished, the jobless, or those racial minorities who are prevented from moving to other sections of the community by prejudice. The blighted areas of the city require the heaviest fire protection, policing, and welfare activity. Owen has noted that 20% of our nation's largest cities are slums, which contribute 6% of the property tax revenue, but take 45% of the costs of municipal government.[10] The only positive aspect of blight, says one study, is that it plays a dynamic role in the community by providing low-cost rental space for new firms.[11]

Commercial activity has moved from the core city to service the new suburbia, and the result has been a steady decline in the percentage of SMSA retail sales accounted for by the central

[10] Owen, p. 23.

[11] Mark Reinsberg, *Growth and Change in Metropolitan Areas and Their Relation to Metropolitan Transportation—A Research Summary* (Chicago: Northwestern University, 1961), p. 20.

business district.[12] Sternlieb has recently analyzed department store trends in Philadelphia, Pittsburgh, and Boston and concluded that the restoration of the primacy of the downtown department store depends heavily on improved mass transit.[13]

Urban Renewal vs. Decentralization

The fiscal strains on the city and state governments have placed the burden of combating blight on the federal government. It has responded by financing up to two thirds the cost of urban renewal programs. The task of central city redevelopment will be enormous, for many of the problems of blight are sociological and will not be solved simply by demolition, bricks, and mortar.

It is not the purpose of this study to recommend the appropriate land use pattern for our largest cities. It is enough to note that a great deal of diversity of opinion exists, both as to the "best" land use and as to the relationship between different land uses and mass transit.

One group, which has tended to become more influential, holds that continued decentralization will "ruin . . . much of the urban economy."[14] This group supports large-scale renewal of our central business districts and central cities. It warns against rebuilding cities exclusively around parking lots and expressways, pointing out that only mass (particularly rapid) transit has the peak-hour capacity to deliver the large numbers of persons necessary to support intensive land use. Therefore this group recommends a balanced transportation network of roads and transit.[15]

Others disagree, particularly as to the role of mass transit. They

[12] In the 12 sample cities this percentage dropped 4 to 8 points during the decade 1948–1958, to levels ranging from 16.3% to 7.8%. See Samuel C. McMillan, "Changing Position of Retail Trade in Central Business Districts," *Traffic Quarterly*, XI (July 1957), pp. 357–372, and "Recent Trends in the Decentralization of Retail Trade," *Traffic Quarterly*, XVI (January, 1962), pp. 79–80.

[13] Sternlieb, p. 19.

[14] Jean Gottman, *Megalopolis* (New York: Twentieth Century Fund, 1961), p. 688.

[15] For example see R. L. Bowersox (ed.), *America is Going Places* (Erie: General Electric, 1962). The planners tend to emphasize the importance of

point out that except for New York City, "the national commercial capital" and perhaps one or two major regional capitals, there will be relatively little CBD growth in comparison with continued decentralization. Further, they believe that decentralization is independent of mass (including rapid) transit, and as highways catch up with the decentralized land use, automobiles, augmented by buses, will be sufficient to handle future travel demands. Therefore, they strongly advise against investment in fixed rail rapid transit facilities in most urban areas.[16]

Vernon notes "instead of wondering how to haul people to and from the CBD with comfort and dispatch, our prime question may well be how to move people from the dispersed homes in one suburb to the dispersed plants in another."[17]

Finally, Owen adds that though intensive development of urban land is important for the economic health of the region, it also makes the community more susceptible to nuclear attack.[18]

Topography

The topography of a region helps create a density of trip patterns conducive to mass transit operations. It is not surprising that New York City, severely limited by topography, early turned to subways and elevateds to carry traffic down the spine of Manhattan and across the East River to Brooklyn and Queens. Similarly, San Francisco, with its bay crossings, has found it easier to sell rapid transit to the community than Los Angeles, which has less disrupting topographical barriers.

Changes in Employment and Recreation Patterns

The trend to a shorter work week has had a severe impact on transit patronage. Saturday used to be transit's peak day, for work trips were augmented by shoppers. Today, Saturday's traffic is about 60% of a normal weekday. As labor's demands for a

---

the CBD, the waste of space taken up by intown parking lots, and the inability of the automobile to carry heavy volumes of rush-hour traffic as compared to rapid transit. However, they note the importance of the automobile for off-peak and suburban traffic.

[16] Meyer et. al., pp. vi–viii.

[17] Vernon, "The Economics and Finances of the Large Metropolis," p. 43.

[18] Owen, p. 21.

shorter work week are met, transit's imbalance between peak and off-peak loads will increase.

Television, home workshops and gardens, and the casualness of suburban living have reduced the desire to make recreational trips away from home. These adverse trends will continue and cut mass transit's off-peak travel. Only major revitalization of downtown cultural and recreational activities will produce the recreational trip desires which transit may be able to exploit.

The Impact of the Automobile

The technological development of the automobile has had as great an effect in destroying the mass transit industry as the streetcar had in creating it. Passenger car registrations have grown from the turn of the century, dipping only during the depression and World War II. There are now about 68.5 million passenger cars registered in the United States, and this figure is expected to rise to 100.6 million by 1980.[19]

Automobile use has increased steadily with ownership. Smith predicts an aggregate increase in automobile vehicle miles of 75% by 1980.[20] Such forecasts, based on the dynamic growth of automobile usage, have convinced many planners that the future city will be dominated by the automobile simply because people have an overwhelming desire to travel in their own cars.

One authority on motivational research has cited compelling reasons for the phenomenon of intensive automobile usage:

> The most important symbol of middle class development in the world today is the automobile. It is the automobile which represents achievement and personal freedom for the middle class. . . . The automobile is the symbol of mobility; the automobile has become the self mobile.[21]

---

[19] Automobile Manufacturers Association, *Automobile Facts & Figures,* 1964 Edition (Detroit: By the Association, 1964), p. 18. [Hereafter cited as *Automobile Facts.*] Forecast contained in Smith & Associates, p. 201.

[20] Smith & Associates, p. 201. The percentage of urban vehicle miles is expected to rise from the present 48% to slightly over 60%. *Doyle Report,* p. 589, and Smith & Associates, p. 201.

[21] Ernest Dichter, "The World Customer," *Harvard Business Review,* 40 (July–August 1962), pp. 118–119.

If this analysis is correct, then mass transit will become a sort of charitable institution providing service for the segment of the public which does not have access to an automobile. Yet, there is growing evidence that the automobile's psychological grip over the driver is not so strong as to prevent him from making a rational modal choice between modern mass transit and the automobile. The aforementioned urban transportation studies have developed correlations which indicate that transit can attract substantial numbers of automobile drivers if it provides fast, comfortable, and convenient service at low cost. These correlations are important, for factors such as comfort and speed are clearly within the control of transit management, in contrast to the external indirect variables, income, population density, land use, and automobile ownership.[22]

The Government as an External Indirect Pressure

The recent engineering-oriented transportation studies have, without question, added much to our understanding of urban travel habits. In the author's opinion, however, they have been somewhat deficient in failing to analyze more closely a major variable in the urban transportation model, government policy. Unfortunately, public policy does not lend itself to translation into ogive curves or mathematical formulae. It is a product of that often maligned word "politics" and represents the fusion of a variety of interests. Therefore, this study will pay particular attention to the place of government and its policies of promotion, regulation, and pressure. Government policy will first be examined as an indirect external pressure on transit through its promotion of highways and commuter railroads.

The Highway Program

If the 19th century can be characterized as the Age of Railroads, the 20th will go down in history as the Age of Highways.

---

[22] For an excellent recent treatment of the science of traffic and transportation forecasting see Martin, Memmott, and Bone, *Principles and Techniques of Predicting Future Demand for Urban Area Transportation*, pp. 116–122,

Between 1921 and 1964 over $199 billion was invested by the federal, state, and local governments in highways. The Association of American Railroads has estimated that only $115 billion of this amount has been recovered through user charges.[23]

The highway program was accelerated by the 1956 Federal Aid Highway Act, which provided for 90% federal financing of the 41,000-mile interstate expressway system. Forty-five percent of the $41 billion cost of the interstate network will be for urban expressways. By 1961 aggregate yearly highway spending rose from $7 billion (1955) to over $12 billion. It is estimated that between 1956 and 1971 over $29 billion will be spent on urban roads and expressways under the Federal primary, secondary, and interstate programs.[24] This massive expenditure should raise our urban expressway mileage from 2,875 (1960) to 9,200 miles. Smith estimates, however, that at least 13,600 miles of urban expressways will be needed to satisfy the nation's urban travel needs.[25]

The federal-state urban expressway network is now being augmented by state toll roads.[26] Historically, toll roads (except for bridges and tunnels) primarily served rural areas; however in 1962 the Massachusetts Turnpike Authority began construction of a $215 million twelve-mile extension of its turnpike into the core area of Boston. This road should go far to resolving the question of whether an expensive urban expressway can be self-supporting through user charges.

It seems clear that if the urban expressway program continues,

---

which discusses the forecasting of mass transit patronage and contrasts the "automobile-residential density" method with the "time diversion curve" approach.

23 Association of American Railroads, Bureau of Railway Economics, *Government Expenditures for Construction Operation, and Maintenance of Transport Facilities by Air, Highway, and Waterway* (Washington: By the Association, 1964), p. 8.

24 U.S. Congress, House, Committee on Ways and Means, *Final Report of the Highway Cost Allocation Study, Parts I–V*, 87th Cong., 1st Sess., 1961, H.R. 54, pp. 55–56. [Hereafter cited as *Highway Cost Allocation Study*.]

25 Smith & Associates, p. 325.

26 For an excellent review of toll roads and their financing, see Francis S. Doody, "The Economics of Toll Roads," *Traffic Quarterly*, XVI (October 1962), pp. 469–487.

as it has in the past, to serve only the needs of the automobile, public policy will have dictated mass transit's fate. The core city will become an "automobile city," which transit cannot profitably serve.

There are strong forces working through the political process promoting the automobile, expressways, and parking garages. These include the American Automobile Association and other public groups representing the driving public, the Automobile Manufacturers Association representing automobile-oriented industries, and those engineers and planners who feel strongly that expressways will solve the urban transportation problem.[27]

Although these groups have been very successful, as evidenced especially in the 1956 Highway Act, in promoting highway construction, they are encountering pressures at the federal and local levels, which may produce modifications in the highway program.

A major change in federal policy, stimulated by President John F. Kennedy's 1962 Transportation Message, has been a change in the law which will require all federally aided highway projects in urban areas of 50,000 or more population after July 1, 1965, to conform to a comprehensive urban transportation plan, which considers both automobiles and mass transit.

There has been also a growing concern by city administrators of the effects of highways on land use and taxes. Although proponents of highways have written at length on increased land values following construction of expressways,[28] some mayors in

[27] The Automobile Manufacturers Association in its various publications is quick to point out the importance of the automobile in our economy. One firm in every six is directly dependent on manufacturing, distribution, and servicing of automobiles. Likewise, one of every seven wage earners is connected with the automobile industry. *Automobile Facts,* 1964, pp. 64–65.

[28] See Smith & Associates, pp. 244–268, 307–316, and *Highway Cost Allocation Study: Part VI.* The latter study concluded that there seemed to be positive advantages over and above savings in transportation costs, although no precise measures of these nonvehicular benefits from expressways could be obtained (p. 78). Proponents of rapid transit also have claimed that rapid transit increases land values. It seems reasonable to conclude that any transportation improvement which attracts traffic will stimulate land development and land value.

our largest cities have begun to protest the disappearance of taxable property to highways, interchanges, and parking areas. The most vocal of these groups was the American Municipal Association, formed in 1959 by mayors and railroad officials, to lobby for a balanced transportation system.

Some urban planners have begun to be alarmed at the increased costs of urban highways. Price tags of $8 to $10 million a mile are not uncommon, and Boston's Central Artery cost over $41 million per mile.[29] Highway advocates quickly point out that in terms of cost per anticipated vehicle mile, the urban highway costs are not unreasonable, especially in comparison with rural highway costs per vehicle mile.

Finally, there has been an anti-expressway movement at the grass roots level, primarily directed at the issue of residential relocation. Boston, in the best "Tea Party" tradition, is the site of the most successful example of local politics defying the planners. All of the recent highway studies recommend an inner belt expressway, but the communities in its path have successfully stalled its construction for more than five years.

It appears that our urban expressway network in our major cities will continue to grow and be improved, but in view of the present federal policies and local pressures it will do so in an atmosphere more favorable to mass transit than in the past.

Promotion of Commuter Railroads

To the observer of urban transportation, the decline of the commuter railroad has been even more striking than has mass transit.[30] The basic problems of railroad commuter service are

[29] See Owen, p. 49, and "Tide Turns for Transit," *Business Week,* October 20, 1962, p. 84.

[30] For concise descriptions and analyses of the decline of rail commutation see George W. Hilton, "The Decline of Railroad Commutation," *Business History Review,* XXXVI (Summer 1962), pp. 171–187, and *Doyle Report,* pp. 553–582, 626–628. Other sources include *Collapse of Commuter Service;* Institute of Public Administration, *Suburbs to Grand Central; A Study of the Feasibility of Reorganizing the Suburban Services of the New York Central and New Haven Railroads Under a Public Agency* (New York: By the Institute, 1963), and U.S. Congress, Senate, Committee on Interstate and Foreign Commerce, *Commuter Transportation,* prepared for the Committee by Anthony Arpaia and the Regional Plan Association, 87th Cong., 1st Sess., 1961.

declining patronage, high costs of operation (particularly labor), high fare structure, and poor downtown distribution facilities.[31]

Today, the only extensive commuter railroad operations are in the New York City, Philadelphia, Chicago, and Boston urban areas. In each city except Chicago the commuter railroads have received state, federal, or local aid. In the cases of Philadelphia and Boston, aid in the form of subsidizing lower fares and increased service has succeeded in increasing patronage but at a subsidy cost of over 25 cents per ride per passenger.[32]

Except perhaps in New York City and Chicago, it appears certain that the commuter train will disappear unless capital and probably operating subsidies are provided.[33] Such aid will depend on the recommendations of the federally supported area transportation studies now in progress.

It is clear that mass transit will either benefit from or be further weakened by further government promotion of commuter railroads. If the railroads are subsidized, they are certain to divert mass transit riders as well as motorists. Thirty percent of the "new" patronage of Philadelphia's subsidized "Operation Northwest" commuter service came from the local transit company.[34]

[31] Even the most efficient versions of railroad commuter service find profitability difficult. Between 1959 and 1962 the Chicago & Northwestern Railroad invested $40 million to replace its aged commuter fleet with 210 double deck, push-pull commuter cars. In 1961 the road reported a deficit from commuter operations of $1.9 million, in large part because of the opening of a paralleling expressway. By 1963 the deficit was replaced by a $203,000 profit, but even this was most likely attributable to traffic gained from the abandoned North Shore electric line. See *Trains*, XXIV (April 1964), p. 6.

[32] Statement of Merritt Taylor, Jr., President, Philadelphia Suburban Transportation Company (Red Arrow Lines) and Commonwealth of Massachusetts, *Mass Transportation Commission Demonstration Project Progress Report Number 5-Tentative Conclusions* (Boston: By the Commission, 1963), p. 19.

[33] For example, in their final report the Massachusetts Mass Transportation Commission reported an increase in ridership of 29% on the Boston & Maine Railroad following a year of increased commuter service and lower fares. However, at the end of the experiment, the railroad immediately petitioned for complete abandonment of all passenger service, claiming annual losses in excess of $2.0 million notwithstanding a $2.2 million subsidy.

[34] City of Philadelphia, Urban Traffic & Transportation Board, *Analysis of Operation Northwest* (Philadelphia: By the Board, 1960).

On the other hand, if commuter railroads are permitted to abandon money-losing operations, it may well be advisable in terms of patronage and costs (particularly capital and operating costs per peak-hour passenger) to convert commuter rail lines to rapid transit operations as was done in Boston (see Chapter 6).

Summary

This chapter has presented a framework for identifying the external pressures confronting the transit industry as well as a list of strategies available to transit management to meet these pressures. The chapter has gone on to discuss the trends and impact of the external indirect pressures, noting the important changes in population, land use, the work week, recreational habits, the use of the automobile, and government promotion of the highways and commuter railroads.

It is not surprising, as confirmed in the responses to the questionnaire, that management at times seems helpless and overwhelmed in the face of the external indirect pressures.

Yet it is the opinion of the author that management in the transit industry has the potential to improve greatly the status of mass transit in the face of this seemingly hostile environment. This can be done through the planning and implementation of strategies aimed at the direct external pressures shown on the chart. These pressures and possible management strategies will be the subject of the next chapter.

CHAPTER 4

Direct External Pressures and Management Strategy

Introduction

This chapter will review each of the direct external pressures shown on the flow chart in the previous chapter (Figure 3.1) and thus set the stage for the analysis of the marketing case studies in the remainder of this book. A brief analysis of potential management strategies will immediately follow the treatment of each of the pressures.

Government Pressure and Political Strategy

Government Promotion

Local Promotion: One official remarked to the author during his field trip, "There is nothing so local as local transit." Insofar as promotion is concerned, he is correct, for until recently the promotion of mass transportation has been exclusively a local function. City credit built most of the rapid transit facilites in New York City, Philadelphia, Boston, and Chicago. During the first quarter of the 20th century such promotion made sense, not only because it permitted faster circulation of people, but because the increase in land values along the rapid transit facility frequently offset the promotional cost to the city. Unfortunately, today city credit must be used for a variety of purposes, and except in New York City, and to a lesser extent in Chicago, Boston, and Philadelphia, transit's priority is low.[1]

Promotion at the State Level: At the state level of government, in contrast to the highway program, there has been little transit aid. Generally, the furthest that the states have gone is to create transit authorities to purchase and operate private transit systems. These authorities have had to cover all expenses from the farebox and cannot draw on state funds for capital or operating expenses.

This historical pattern has been changed during the past two years by several noteworthy developments. In 1962 New York and New Jersey's Port of New York Authority, which had formerly concentrated its activities on highways, ports, and airports, agreed to invest $150 million to purchase, refurbish, and operate the bankrupt Hudson and Manhattan Railroad.[2] Again, the funds come from the revenues collected by the autonomous authority, not the state. New Jersey and Pennsylvania's Delaware River Port Authority approved in early 1962 a $62 million extension of its Philadelphia-Camden rapid transit line. Construction began in mid-1964.

But the most dramatic development in 1962 was the approval in November by the voters of the San Francisco Bay Area Rapid

[1] The debt service charges on rapid transit bonds held by the city of New York totaled $104.6 million during the fiscal year ending June 1963. In addition, the city paid the transit authority for police services, school differentials, and power as shown in Table 2.4. As of 1961 the Chicago Transit Authority was responsible for about $21 million of the $110 million cost of the subway system. The remainder was borne by: City of Chicago, $53.9 million; Cook County, $3 million; State of Illinois, $6.3 million; and a PWA grant of $26 million. Until 1964 the city of Boston and 13 cities and towns surrounding the core were responsible for absorbing 100% of the operating and capital deficits of the Metropolitan Transit Authority. Annual deficits have run as high as $21 million. Philadelphia's transit improvement program encompassing both grants and funding to be repaid by the transit company is outlined in City of Philadelphia, Department of Public Property, *Philadelphia's Capital Program for Transit Operations, 1961–1965* (Philadelphia: By the Department, 1961), p. 16.

[2] Institute for Rapid Transit, *Newsletter* III (October 19, 1962), p. 5. [Hereafter cited as IRT, *Newsletter.*]

Transit District of a $792 million general obligation bond issue to finance the majority of the cost of a $997.6 million rapid transit system. The State of California is offering significant assistance by providing an additional $132,720,000 for the trans-bay subway tube from surplus automobile tolls collected for the San Francisco-Oakland Bay Bridge. The remainder of the capital cost and the future operating expenses are expected to be covered by system revenues.[3]

Most recently the Commonwealth of Massachusetts enacted legislation in June 1964 creating the Massachusetts Bay Transportation Authority (MBTA) to administer a statewide $225 million program of aid to mass transit companies and commuter railroads. The state agreed to increase the cigarette tax by 2 cents per pack and use the revenues to help finance the cost of the program. It is expected that the new legislation will enable the Boston transit system to expand its existing rapid transit routes into the suburbs (see Chapter 6). The legislation enabled the MBTA to acquire Boston's Metropolitan Transit Authority (MTA) and expanded the 14-city and town MTA district to 78 cities and towns in the Boston metropolitan region. Unlike the former 14-city and town district, the 78 cities and towns will bear only a portion of the capital costs but will continue to be responsible for any operating deficits resulting from MBTA transit service in the Boston area. It should be noted that throughout this study, the title Metropolitan Transit Authority is used in discussing the Boston transit system, inasmuch as the MBTA came into existence after the author's field work.

Promotion at the Federal Level: As recently as 1955 a government report sanctioned the historical policy of federal disinterest in mass transit, saying that transit was either a state or a local problem.[4] The inability of the states and municipalities to

[3] The initial plan for the Bay Area Rapid Transit District proposed a five county system costing $1.2 billion. Two of the five counties withdrew from the District. For details of the financial and organizational structure see *Senate, Urban Mass Transit, 1962,* pp. 145–150. A more recent summary of progress on the Bay Area system can be found in IRT, *Newsletter* IV (December 15, 1963), pp. 8–36.

[4] William Miller, *Metropolitan Rapid Transit Financing,* p. 25.

finance transit improvements, plus the deterioration of railroad commuter and transit service, created strong pressures for federal aid.

A transit aid bill was introduced into Congress in 1960 and passed the Senate but not the House. Following strong pressure, however, Congress incorporated a program of transit planning grants, demonstration grants, and loans into the Housing Act of 1961. But there was no favorable action taken on the plea for capital aid for projects such as rapid transit lines.[5]

In 1962 legislation was introduced to provide $500 million in capital aid over a three-year period to the transit industry. The aid was contingent on: (1) the community possessing or actively developing a comprehensive transportation plan based on future land use and economic activity;[6] (2) the project in question conforming to this plan; (3) approval of the grant by the Housing and Home Finance Agency; (4) administration of the grant by a public agency, which could either lease to private companies or operate the capital facilities; and (5) the raising of one third of the "net project cost" by state or local appropriations.[7] In addi-

[5] See *Senate, Urban Mass Transit, 1962*, pp. 76, 78. The Act authorized a transit loan fund of $50 million and a demonstration grant fund of $25 million. Demonstration grants were predicated on the existence of a community transportation plan, and were to be financed by two-thirds federal funds, one-third local funds. The 1962 appropriations cut the combined loan and demonstration program to $42.5 million.

[6] For statements on the critical importance of planning see *Doyle Report*, pp. 621–625, and statement of Luther Gulick, president of the Institute of Public Administration in U.S., Congress, Senate, Committee on Banking and Currency, *Hearings, Urban Mass Transportation*, 87th Cong., 1st Sess., 1961, p. 256. Gulick noted that if horizontal urban transportation systems could be planned and operated like vertical systems, e.g., elevators, much of the urban transportation problem would be solved. Vertical systems are characterized by (1) continual technical improvement, (2) automation, (3) integrated financing with buildings and no user charges, and (4) planned in relation to the expected movement of persons and goods to the floors in the building.

[7] "Net project cost" would be that portion of the total project capital cost which could not be supported by expected revenues. In communities where an urgent need existed, but planning was incomplete, the federal government's share of the "net project cost" would be reduced from two thirds to one half. The 50–50 "emergency grant" authorization would terminate in three years.

tion, the bill provided for continuance of the 1961 loan program, an increase in the demonstration and planning funds, relocation payments to those affected by mass transit projects, and a strong statement emphasizing the need for coordination on housing, highways, and transit.

The proposed Urban Mass Transit Act of 1962 had the strong legislative sponsorship of Senator Harrison Williams (D. New Jersey) and executive support in President John F. Kennedy's 1962 Transportation Message. In addition, the American Municipal Association, individual mayors, the AFL-CIO, and even a petroleum company were among those who testified in favor of the bill.

On the other hand, there was disagreement within the transit industry over the provisions of the bill. O. Roy Chalk, President of Washington's D.C. Transit Company, asked that direct grants and the authority for transit planning be given to private companies.[8] The spokesman for the American Transit Association, though supporting the concept of federal aid, reported that several other private companies feared the administration of grants and loans by local public bodies.[9] One prominent and respected transit executive resigned from the American Transit Association following its endorsement of federal aid, saying, "To force people in Blue Bump, Mississippi, to pay in their taxes for the failures of transit to break even or make a profit . . . is immoral legalized robbery."[10]

Several strong interest groups testified against the bill. The U.S. Chamber of Commerce claimed that urban transportation was not a national problem and did not warrant federal aid.[11] This view was supported by certain Congressmen opposed to heavy federal spending. The American Farm Bureau Federation also protested the need for federal aid, saying that it would be

[8] *Senate, Urban Mass Transit, 1962*, pp. 481, 483.

[9] U.S., Congress, House, Committee on Banking & Currency, Subcommittee #3, Hearings, Urban Mass Transportation Act, 87th Cong., 2d Sess., 1962, pp. 761–767. [Hereafter cited as *House, Urban Mass Transit, 1962.*]

[10] Paul Ditmar, "Letter to the Editor," *Metropolitan Transportation*, LVIII (February 1962), p. 11.

[11] *House, Urban Mass Transit, 1962*, pp. 581–608.

"inflationary and harmful to the general interest."[12] Finally, the American Road Builders Association warned against any measure which might lead to cutbacks in the highway program.[13]

In addition to the above resistance, there was some evidence that the transit industry had not exploited fully the aid it received in the Housing Act of 1961. Table 4.1 shows the demonstration projects approved by the Housing and Home Finance Agency as of January 1964. During 1962 over 75% of the demonstration grants were used to improve railroad commuter service. Out of a total of $11.0 million spent by the federal and local governments on the projects in 1962, only $1.2 million was used for mass transportation experiments in the twelve sample cities. One reason for this disparity was that some transit companies had no way of obtaining the 33⅓% local contribution necessary to receive federal funds. Another problem was that some of the transit industry proposals required capital aid, which was specifically excluded from the 1961 Act.[14]

During 1963 transit's performance was much better. The percentages were almost reversed, primarily because of major grants to San Francisco and Pittsburgh for experiments with new rapid transit equipment. By January 1964 the total $30.4 million in demonstration projects was split almost 50–50 between commuter railroads and mass transit. But even so, in comparison with the commuter railroads, relatively small amounts of funds were allocated for the improvement of existing transit service.

After extensive hearings and favorable committee reports, the 1962 bill was pigeonholed until 1963. In April 1963 the Senate passed transit aid legislation similar to the 1962 bill except: (1) the capital aid fund was cut from $500 million to $375 million; (2) aid to any one state was restricted to a maximum of 12.5% of the grant funds; (3) clauses for the protection of labor were inserted; and (4) the federal government was permitted to guaran-

12 *Senate, Urban Mass Transit, 1962,* pp. 314–320.

13 *Ibid.,* pp. 494–497. For an excellent discussion of the highway pressure groups active in the transit aid struggle, see *Congressional Quarterly Weekly Report,* XXI (Week ending October 4, 1963), pp. 1727–1737.

14 *Senate, Urban Mass Transit, 1962,* p. 121, and Institute for Rapid Transit, *A Report to the Nation, Proceedings of First Annual Meeting* (Washington: By the Institute, 1962), p. 68.

tee up to 75% of the value of revenue bonds (not to exceed $375 million) issued to finance capital projects. The latter feature was sought by those autonomous transit authorities which were not permitted by law to raise the required one third of the "net project cost" through taxes. Although the House also reported a transit bill out of Committee in April 1963, the measure was not brought to the floor for a vote because of an alleged lack of grass roots support[15] and the resistance by Congress to approve federal aid to urban areas.[16]

By June 1964, however, the strong support of President Johnson and key Representatives led to House approval of a transit bill similar to that passed by the Senate in 1963.[17] The major change was the deletion of the revenue bond guarantee provision. As signed by the President, the Urban Mass Transportation Act of 1964 authorized: (1) extension indefinitely of the $50 million loan fund created by the Housing Act of 1961; (2) capital grants from a $375 million fund to transit projects in conformance with comprehensive urban transportation plans (as in the proposed 1962 legislation, the federal share of the "net project cost" would range from one half to two thirds depending upon the status of the community's transportation plan); (3) federal grants for payment of relocation expenses; (4) use of $30 million of the $375 million for up to 100% federal grants for mass transportation research and development; and (5) continuation of the $25 million 1961 demonstration grant program on a 100% rather than the former two-thirds federal basis. The loans and grants would

[15] In the fall of 1963 Senator Harrison Williams was quoted: "If every commuter whose train was broken down and if every bus rider who has waited 20 or 30 minutes for the bus to come by had written their Congressman, we would have had the legislation passed by now." *Passenger Transport* October 11, 1963, p. 1.

[16] See *Congressional Quarterly Weekly Report*, XXI (Week ending December 20, 1963), p. 2219, for a review of the committee hearings and votes on transit aid. During this session the important Area Redevelopment Bill was pigeonholed in both the Senate and House, following defeat of a similar measure in the House. This action indicated major resistance to increased programs of federal urban aid.

[17] Yet passage of the measure did not come easily. Only a week before the final vote in the House, rumors were that there was only a 50–50 chance of passage. The actual affirmative vote was 212–189.

Table 4.1   **Approved Demonstration Grants:**

Description of Project	Location of Project	Date Approved
1. Increase local bus service	Detroit, Mich.	3/27/62
2. Study monorail operation	Seattle, Wash.	6/29/62
3. Improve service, add new routes, and reduce fares	Massachusetts	9/28/62
4. Improve frequency of service and reduce fares	Philadelphia, Pa.	10/22/62
5. Add new routes to suburbs	Memphis, Tenn.	12/ 4/62
6. New station and parking lot	New Brunswick, N.J.	12/17/62
Sub Total 1962		
7. Test equipment for automatic fare collection	Two stations on Long Island Railroad	1/10/63
8. Downtown shuttle service using small buses and low fares	Washington, D.C.	1/24/63
9. Test use of computers in scheduling transit service	Kansas State University	4/26/63
10. Finance analytical studies of rail commuter service	Philadelphia, Pa.	6/12/63
11. Determine feasibility of lightweight low capacity rapid transit vehicles	Pittsburgh, Pa.	6/15/63
12. Provide faster, more frequent rail commuter service and increase parking facilities	Westchester and Putnam County, New York	6/18/63
13. Demonstrate and test new concepts in rapid transit equipment design	San Francisco, Cal.	6/18/63
14. Establish new bus routes	Nashville, Tenn.	6/21/63
15. Study commuter railroad operations and implement improved service	Queens-Nassau sector of Greater New York City	6/21/63
16. Increase feeder bus service to commuter railroad station	Rockland County, New York	6/21/63
Sub Total 1963		
17. Initiate rapid transit service over abandoned interurban electric railroad	Chicago, Illinois	1/21/64
Grand Total All Projects		

SOURCES: *Housing and Home Finance Agency* and *Institute for Rapid Transit.*

Housing and Home Finance Agency, as of January 1964
(In thousands)

Mass Transit		RR. Commuter		Totals	
Total Cost	Federal Share	Total Cost	Federal Share	Total Cost	Federal Share
$ 336.6	$ 224.4	—	—	$ 336.6	$ 224.4
15.0	10.0			15.0	10.0
2,000.0[1]	1,333.0	$ 3,400.0	$ 2,267.0	5,400.0	3,600.0
		4,674.0	3,116.0	4,674.0	3,116.0
291.7	194.5			291.7	194.5
		256.2	170.8	256.2	170.8
2,643.3	1,761.9	8,330.2	5,553.8	10,973.5	7,315.7
		272.1	181.4	272.1	181.4
240.7	160.5			240.7	160.5
18.7	12.5			18.7	12.5
		437.5	291.7	437.5	291.7
3,170.0	2,113.0			3,170.0	2,113.0
		1,948.6	1,299.1	1,948.6	1,299.1
7,329.0	4,886.0			7,329.0	4,886.0
600.0	400.0			600.0	400.0
		4,778.0	3,185.0	4,778.0	3,185.0
148.7	99.2			148.7	99.2
11,507.1	7,671.2	7,436.2	4,957.1	18,943.4	12,628.4
523.8	349.2			523.8	349.2
$14,674.2	$9,782.3	$15,766.4	$10,510.9	$30,440.7	$20,293.3

[1] Of this amount, Boston's Metropolitan Transit Authority received only $900,000. The remainder of the "mass transportation" funds were used for projects involving suburban or small city bus lines.

be administered by the Housing and Home Finance Agency. The Act stipulated that transit workers be protected and that no state receive more than 12.5% of the funds appropriated for mass transportation projects, and it barred federal financial assistance to acquire private transit companies unless the Administrator of the Housing and Home Finance Agency determined that the purchase was vital to the realization of a coordinated mass transportation system.

The Urban Mass Transportation Act of 1964 was a tremendous victory for the transit industry. Yet, if the $10 billion estimate of industry capital needs is accurate, the $375 million in capital aid, limited to $46.9 million per state, will be exhausted quickly, and the industry will be forced to return again "to the Hill" for aid in the future. In view of the experience of 1961–1964, it would seem that future industry successes in obtaining capital aid at the federal level will depend upon the ability (1) to agree within the industry (through its trade association) on the kind of legislation desired; (2) to obtain strong support from the legislative and executive branches of the government; (3) to supply useful information to the legislative branch of the government in support of legislation;[18] (4) to form alliances with other groups who might stand to benefit from improved mass transit; (5) to broaden the base of public support through grass roots campaigns; and (6) when partial aid is obtained, to show tangible evidence to the legislators and the public that the aid is being used effectively.

Government Regulation

The history of government regulation of the mass transit industry is well summarized in Mossman's study.[19] In return for a franchise to operate over urban routes, a private company had to submit to regulation of fares, service, finance, and even equipment. Regulation could be vested in either the city or state, and sometimes, as in Philadelphia, in a combination of both.

18 For example, see *Collapse of Commuter Service*. This study was quoted frequently during the 1961 debates on aid to transit and commuter railroads. One of its most publicized findings was that $31 billion would have to be spent on highways if railroad commuter service was abandoned in five major cities.

19 See note 4, Chapter 2.

Although an extensive review of regulation of mass transit would be out of place in this study, it seems reasonable to conclude that the regulatory process was at its best when protecting the public against clear violations of its interest by private management.[20] Unfortunately the regulatory process sometimes became a political device, particularly before elections, to delay or even prevent fare increases or cuts in service. At such times, a strong case could be made to end all regulation, in view of the fact that transit's monopoly of urban travel ceased with the coming of the automobile.

The regulatory process continues to affect heavily the operations of major private companies, such as those in Philadelphia and Washington, D.C., but its role in our largest cities is being superseded by the autonomous authorities and transit districts.

Government Pressure

Political pressure in the mass transit industry can be defined as the effort by elected or appointed public officials to produce a change in transit policy by threatening to invoke power. This process may be a formal one, for example, legislative vote, executive order, power of appointment; or an informal one, that is, carried on through negotiations, conferences, confrontations, etc., supported by political and economic threats. The transition from private to public enterprise has produced a change in the character and effectiveness of political pressure.

Private Companies: Private companies are most subject to political pressure during the course of the regulatory process and labor negotiations. An appeal to the courts can reverse clearly unfair regulatory decisions, but more often the reluctance of the courts to review regulatory proceedings leaves the companies exposed to political power.

[20] See John Bauer and Peter Costello, *Transit Modernization and Street Traffic Control* (Chicago: Public Administration Service, 1950), p. 210, which condemned policies of some private companies: "Unfortunately, most [private] companies have the private profit attitude, which embodies the background of corporate ownership and control, and is commonly accentuated by private speculative goals. . . . In any such [speculative] interest, the management is constrained to pursue the highest attainable profits and is inevitably entangled with the speculative engagements of the controlling group; it is under incessant conflict between public service [and] speculative aims."

In more serious situations such as a strike, political power uses its ultimate weapon, revocation of the franchise and condemnation of the property. In 1962 the mayor of New York City, angered by threats of private management to raise fares, as well as determined to end a strike quickly, convinced the state legislature to revoke the franchise of the Fifth Avenue Coach Lines.[21] But the more common form of political pressure during wage negotiations is a suggested settlement in return for a less adamant stand by the city in future fare increase proceedings.

It seems quite probable that federal aid will add to these pressures. Before and after money is granted, there will be extended discussions between company and public officials on major policy issues such as fares, service, and equipment. Such a prospect should not alarm private management, for it is axiomatic that the provider of funds has a say as to their use. The industry has long been used to bankers, and sometimes representatives of the city, sitting in its directors' meetings.

Public Companies: Public companies are exposed to political pressure in all phases of their operations: fares, service, finance, extensions, labor relations, executive appointments, and at times promotion of personnel.

Pressure for lower fares and better service by the mayor's office, city council, or even state legislature is often stronger toward public (even those not supported by tax funds) than private companies, since the very concept of "public" company seems to imply extra service. In theory, such pressure cannot be criticized, particularly when the company is subsidized by taxes, for transit policy should be responsive to the public's wishes. The trouble begins when executive and legislative interference takes the form of inconsistent statements and votes, such as "The deficit will be reduced; workers will not be fired; fares will not be raised; service will not be cut."[22]

Political power may be the by-product of legislation which established the public companies. In some cases, what was for-

21 See *New York Times,* March 2–29, 1962.

22 It should not be inferred that all legislative interference is bad. Often studies undertaken by legislative committees may be quite helpful to the transit executive board in formulating long- and short-range policy.

merly handled through the regulatory process is now directly vested in the approval of legislative bodies or the electorate.

Again, as in the case of private companies, federal financial aid will further complicate the patterns of political power and pressure.

But the distinguishing feature of the public company is the composition and policies of the executive board. Although at the outset of public ownership, boards contain representatives of the business, legal, and financial communities, thus blending qualified personnel with an executive policy of the "public" rather than private interest, their successors sometimes reflect straight political appointments.

This infusion of politics directly into the top policy-making level of the transit company can have several unfortunate consequences. Frequent appointments of individuals with no transit experience to the boards can create friction with the career operating officials, who must teach the new board member "the business from the ground up."[23] This observation assumes even greater importance in view of the peculiar position of the executive board in the transit industry. In theory, the chief administrative officer and his staff should run the company on a day-to-day basis under major policy directives issued by an executive board. By being a member of that board, the chief administrative officer, in turn, participates in the determination of major policies. But in the transit industry, major policy decisions occur relatively infrequently. For example, price changes may not take place for as long as three years. Specifications for new equipment may remain unchanged for seven or eight years, and the interval between new maintenance facilities may be as long as twenty-five years. Since the executive board is not faced with major issues at each meeting, it is not surprising that it sometimes concerns itself with the day-to-day operations of the transit system.

[23] In most cases of public ownership, many of the former operating officials remain, sometimes (e.g. Chicago) by legislative mandate. A new trend has been for professional management (frequently men who administered National City Lines' properties) to run the company under contract, subject to the policies of the executive board. The author's questionnaire (Question 4) found that the average years of transit experience of executive boards of public companies was five, versus eighteen in private companies.

The resulting difficulties in determining authority and responsibility for decisions between the executive board and career operating officials were mentioned to the author by officials in several of the cities he visited.

In the author's opinion, such conflicts can be minimized by insisting that the position of executive board member be a part-time job, in the same manner that boards of directors function in private industry. In turn, this calls for appointments of chief administrative officers with demonstrated executive ability and transit experience, comparable to the president of a company in the private sector of the economy.

But an even greater problem than executive board-career official friction is the possibility that the executive board may implement policies concerning working conditions, service, recruitment, or promotion, which represents the pressures of special interest groups and political power. This concern for the particular rather than the elusive "public interest" was not unknown during the regime of private enterprise. Witness the following criticism:

> There is here, however, the grave difficulty that most companies to a large extent maintain the psychology of ordinary private business and do not really recognize the fact that they are engaged in essential public service. . . . The . . . managements have usually the fixed views of ordinary private business that they must be free to decide policies and to handle the various aspects of transportation without municipal interference or participation. . . . they are commonly disdainful of the "politicians" in the city hall. While they may give lip service to cooperation, actually they are often antagonistic and oppose the changes and improvements that are essential to the advancement of public interest.[24]

What has happened is that the particular interest has shifted from the banker and stockholder to the politician, and the focus of concern from financial to other policies. In both cases, this particular interest can coincide with or thwart the public interest.

Summary—Government Pressure: Mass transit management has always worked in an atmosphere of political pressure. But

[24] Bauer and Costello, *Transport Modernization and Street Traffic,* p. 208.

the transitions from private to public ownership and internal (or bank) to governmental financing have added to the traditional local pressures for better service and lower fares the direct problems of political appointments, legislative interference, and patronage.

The strategy of private companies against political pressures will continue to be recourse to the courts or public exposure of political threats. The managements of public companies will have a more difficult task. Their objectives should be: (1) to insure competent appointments to transit executive boards; (2) to obtain agreement from the executive and legislative branches on major policy issues such as operating the system at a profit; and (3) to protect the company from political patronage.

Autonomous public authorities may find it easier to be insulated from political pressure, because the trust indentures of the revenue bonds require profitable operation. But both autonomous authorities and tax-supported transit districts will have to appeal to a variety of interest groups (e.g., business, civic, press, and government) to insure unhampered operation.

In the battle against government pressure, the stakes are as great as campaigns to obtain government funds. To fail to plan and implement a political strategy against government pressure in an industry which is labor, not capital, intensive can only bring financial disaster and complete lack of public support. This observation leads to one of the more important strategy areas, labor relations.

Labor Pressure and Management Strategy

Labor Pressure

Earlier in this study it was reported that management believed external pressures beyond their control to be their single greatest problem. Significantly, labor pressure was second on their list (Question 2). This is not surprising, for 60% to 70% of the transit revenue dollar is paid out in wages. Labor drives and maintains the vehicles, for the most part unaided by labor-saving devices. The most conspicuous exception is the bus washing machine.

These technological facts of life are matched by the strong bargaining power of the labor unions. The unions developed out of a period when entrepreneurs exploited horsecar drivers with long hours and low pay. As their strength grew, they took advantage of the fact that a transit strike is politically unacceptable, and often found their demands supported by political pressure.

Following the Second World War both public and private transit companies attempted to cut service and manpower to meet declining traffic and rising costs. At times the same political pressures, which contributed to increased labor costs, resisted the cuts in service. Management then attempted to improve the productivity of the workforce by changing historic work rules and pay privileges, and this further increased the resistance from labor. Sometimes disgruntled drivers would retaliate by "running slow" or "bunching up" on their routes, thereby ruining the best schedules and contributing to the transit's unpopularity with the public. In other instances the men would refuse to work overtime. During the period 1960–1963 there were major transit strikes in New York City, Boston, Rochester, and Philadelphia.

In Chapter 2 it was observed that the operating ratios of public companies in 1961 were more unfavorable than those of private companies. The author's questionnaire investigated this relationship and the results are shown in Table 4.2.

The responses show that for the most part the public and private executives tend to defend their respective forms of ownership and view their counterparts with suspicion. Thus, the public companies feel that the lack of the profit motive is no deterrent to efficiency, but the private companies believe the opposite. In addition, most of the public companies believe that their labor problem is no worse than that of the private companies. Two facts should be emphasized, however. There are exceptions to the above generalizations (one public company believes labor is stronger under public) and many agree that as a company makes the transition from private enterprise through an autonomous transit authority subject to a trust indenture to the tax-supported transit district, the pressures of political patronage increase, and the chances for efficiency diminish.

Table 4.2

Questionnaire Responses:
Attitudes on Efficiency of Public Operations

Do You Agree with the Following?	Yes		No	
	Public	*Private*	*Public*	*Private*
a. Without the profit motive there is little chance for efficiency.	1	3	3	1
b. Publicly operated companies subject to a trust indenture have the same profit motives as private companies, except that they don't pay dividends to stockholders.	4	1	1	3
c. Publicly operated systems *not* subject to a trust indenture tend to be *less* efficient than private companies or public companies subject to a trust indenture.	4	3		
d. Labor unions tend to have more strength under public ownership as contrasted with private.	1	2	4	2
e. Subsidized public systems will find it extremely difficult to resist political pressures with respect to employment.	2	3	2	1

SOURCE: Question 9.

Labor Strategy of Transit Management

Some transit executives hope to solve the labor cost problem through automation in the same manner that elevator operators in office buildings have been replaced by automatic equipment. It appears that both the costs of automation and the political obstacles to its installation will limit its application to the transit industry in the foreseeable future. The New York City transit authority, for example, in 1962 began operation of an automated shuttle train, but the motorman remained in the cab.[25] And automation has not yet solved the bus driver problem, which in

[25] The automated train was destroyed along with other equipment in a disastrous fire April 21, 1964, in the 42d Street shuttle subway.

most companies constitutes the major part of the transportation department's payroll. Automation's most likely role will be in conjunction with completely new rapid transit systems, but even in these cases it will be difficult to prevent the operating union from keeping at least one man on each train.[26]

The labor problem will continue to grow. Short-range solutions will hinge on better utilization of manpower through modifications in the work rules and application of electronic data processing (ADP) to trip scheduling. A strict no-hire policy can reduce excess personnel through attrition. New maintenance facilities should further reduce the need for manpower. Again, the strong support of public officials will be necessary (particularly in the case of public transit companies) if these short-run savings are to be achieved.

On the other hand, the pay of those workers who remain will continue to increase. It can be reasonably concluded that in the absence of widespread automation the total costs of transit operation will continue to rise, largely because of the labor component of those costs.

Recruitment and Executive Development

During informal discussions with transit executives on his field trips, the author received the impression that the decline of transit patronage and the advent of public ownership have reduced the career appeal of the mass transit industry. In view of the importance of management succession, several questions pertaining to the problem of recruitment and executive development were included in the questionnaire.

The first series of questions focused on profile data of top management in the industry. The results are summarized in Table 4.3. The data indicate that the average member of the present top management team has had over 25 years' experience in the industry and, with the exception of the treasurer, is nearing the retirement age. Significantly, a large percentage of

[26] For a more detailed discussion of the future impact of automation, see Lang and Soberman, p. 111 ff.

Table 4.3

Questionnaire Responses:
Profile Data, Transit Management

Nature of Question	*Chief Admin. Officer*	*Supt. of Operations*	*Treas- urer*	*Chief Engineer*
Average age (years)	60	56	49	58
Years' experience in transit industry	28	29	27	31
Location of previous management job:				
Within the company	5	9	9	6
From outside the company	4	—	—	1
Where will next holder of job come from:				
Within the company	2	7	7	4
From outside the company	4	—	—	—
Highest level of education of present holder of job:				
High school or lower	2	3	3	1
College	7	6	6	6
Likely highest level of education of next holder of job:				
High school or lower	1	2	1	—
College	7	6	7	6

SOURCE: Question 4.

today's management are college graduates, and the chief administrative officers look forward to continuing to fill these top level posts from the ranks of college graduates.

On the other hand, a series of questions was asked concerning their recruitment and executive development programs, and the answers (Table 4.4) were not encouraging. An overwhelming majority of the companies have no active management recruiting programs, not only because of the costs of such programs, but also because the majority of top management believes transit does not offer a satisfying career in terms of pay or stimulating activity.

The alternative to developing a cadre of future managerial personnel from college graduates is to train men from within the organization. A properly conceived and implemented em-

Table 4.4

Questionnaire Responses:
Attitudes on Careers and Recruitment

Do You Agree with the Following:	*Yes*	*No*
A young man graduating from college can look forward to a satisfying career in mass transit.	4	5
Your company has an active management *recruiting* program.	1	8
Your company has a formal management *training* program.	5	4
In comparison with other occupations, the members of the management team in mass transit are well paid.	2	6

SOURCE: Question 6.

ployee training and development program might not only insure a supply of managerial talent but also reduce labor militancy, thereby controlling costs and improving service. This is not guaranteed. In 1963 the Philadelphia Transportation Company suffered a major strike in the midst of an intensive program to improve employee relations and develop supervisory talent. Still, only five of the nine companies have formal management training programs.

Perhaps the most important finding was the fact that four of six chief administrative officers recognize that their successors probably will not come from within the organization. Thus, management realizes this problem of succession, but only a few of the companies have been able to take positive steps to meet the problem. If, in fact, the industry stands at the threshold of a renaissance, it will need competent, progressive top management. The author will suggest one approach toward meeting this problem at the end of this study, under the heading of improvements in marketing strategy.

Financial Strategy

As the mass transit industry has undergone the transition from private enterprise through autonomous public authorities to tax-supported transit districts, financial strategy has also shifted. The treasurers of private mass transit companies face the same problems as their counterparts in other service industries (e.g., railroads, airlines). Particular attention is paid to maintaining good relations with the stockholders and banking community.

Autonomous public companies, financed by revenue bonds, show a similar pattern, except that the equity interest is replaced by the bondholder and trust indenture accompanying the revenue bonds. In such cases the treasurer, as well as other officials in the organization, must work closely with independent engineers and financial advisers representing the bondholders. But even though these companies are "public," quite often the profit orientation of private enterprise remains to satisfy the trust indenture. As noted previously, several transit officials agree that an autonomous public authority is much like private enterprise, except that the dividends go to the public in the form of capital improvements.

As the transit industry comes to depend on government promotion for capital aid or operating subsidies, financial strategy must undergo a major change. The world of fiscal appropriations, as noted in the section on government promotion and political strategy, is quite different from that of the banker, and the transit treasurer as well as other top officials will be forced to speak the language of the politician as well as that of the banking community.

Technological Developments and Transit Strategy

Technological Pressures

Major technological developments can be the most critical external variable in an industry's history. The invention of the electric railway created the interurban industry; the automobile destroyed it completely in the space of 35 years. Transit, likewise, may either benefit or be rendered obsolete by technology during the next decades.

Urban transportation technology is moving ahead on three major fronts. The most dramatic are improvements which would obviate trips entirely (e.g., telephone-television communications devices). At the present time the transit industry has little to fear from this source.

Constant research is being undertaken to improve user owned or leased vehicular transportation. One system envisions gathering private automobiles into trains for express trips to the central city. The other approach to improving private automobile transportation is the automated highway.[27] Present evidence indicates that neither of these technologies will be available in large scale during the next two decades.[28]

The final area of technology is concentrating on nonuser owned vehicular transportation. The subjects of this research include high capacity vehicles, low capacity vehicles, and techniques for gathering buses into trains for suburban central city operation.[29]

The only serious contender to the automobile, bus, rapid transit car, and railroad commuter train has been the monorail system of passenger transportation. Although monorails are being constructed in foreign countries for low-volume airport-CBD service, no city has approved the monorail as a component of a high-volume mass transit system. Nor is one likely to do so, for an elevated two-rail system can outperform the monorail.[30] Significantly, the only major rapid transit plan recently approved (San Francisco) relies on high performance two-rail rapid transit cars.[31]

---

[27] There have been numerous articles on technological improvements in urban transit. For a discussion of user-owned improvements see Lawrence R. Hafstad, *A Look Ahead in Highway Transportation* (Detroit: General Motors Research Laboratories, 1961).

[28] *Chicago Area Transportation Study* (Chicago: CATS, 1959–1962), III, p. 5.

[29] See Westinghouse Industrial Systems, *The Westinghouse Transit Expressway* (Pittsburgh, 1962) for discussion of low capacity vehicles; and Herman S. Botzow, *Monorails* (New York: Simmons Boardman, 1960) for both an extensive treatment of monorails and the "uni-bus" concept (p. 50). Other sources of information on mass transit technology are listed in note 12, Chapter 1.

[30] See IRT, *Newsletter,* III (October 19, 1962), and Meyer et. al., p. 80.

[31] The results of the evaluation of monorails vs. "duorails" are reported in IRT, *Newsletter,* V (February 15, 1964), p. 31.

There will, no doubt, be improvements in all phases of our conventional urban transportation system—automobiles, highways, rapid transit, etc.—but these improvements should offset one another. If anything, these improvements should benefit transit in the balance, for its standards of comfort and speed are generally so poor that even unspectacular improvements (in the technological sense), such as escalators and air conditioning, will drastically improve its image.

Research and Development—Transit Industry Cooperation

Until recently research in many transit companies meant anyone in the organization who was tabulating historical data for a variety of purposes. The schedule department might be running a check of transfers, or the comptroller plotting the trend of revenues in preparation for a fare increase. This kind of research is best labeled "market research" and will be discussed under marketing strategy.

A second kind of research pertains to activities which lead to improvements in technology. Unfortunately, except for one period in the late 1930's which culminated in the development of the PCC streamlined streetcar, the industry, in contrast to its competitor, the automobile, has lagged far behind in technological research. The principal reason for this inactivity has been the shortage of industry funds and the reluctance of its suppliers to commit funds for research in view of the seemingly poor future of the industry.

Recently this pessimistic picture has changed for the better. At the insistence of several major transit companies, a "new look" bus was developed to replace a design which had remained almost unchanged for 20 years. The Institute for Rapid Transit has been established by the transit industry to promote and coordinate rapid transit research. Several large suppliers are developing improved rapid transit vehicles.

Less dramatic, but extremely important for efficient transit operation, have been the starts made toward developing automated fare collection devices, electronic data processing for scheduling vehicles, and devices to record passengers at peak-load points and along the routes automatically.

Consumer Demand and Marketing Strategy

Importance of Marketing Strategy

The ultimate purpose of a mass transit company (in the opinion of this author) is not to serve as an expensive standby facility like the fire department, but rather to induce persons making trips within the company's service area to use transit regularly in preference to some other mode of transportation.

Thus far this study has shown that the major transit companies are facing financial crises, resulting from a cost-revenue squeeze. Revenues, despite major fare increases, have remained static or declined as passenger traffic has fallen, whereas labor costs, the largest component of transit expenses, have steadily risen. Even if transit should be able to control labor costs in the short run, the cost-revenue squeeze will remain if traffic continues to decline and fare increases reach the point of diminishing returns. The only long-run solution to the cost-revenue problem, short of operational as well as capital subsidies, will be increased traffic and revenues to support the constantly rising costs. Therefore, marketing strategy assumes major importance in transit management's decision areas, for it is the only strategy shown on the flow chart (Figure 3.1) directly concerned with the problem of maintaining and stimulating demand.

The remainder of this study will focus on a series of case studies of marketing strategy. The cases will be analyzed from three points of view: the individual policies comprising marketing strategy, the interrelationship between marketing and political strategy, and the formal organization for assigning authority and responsibility for marketing strategy. Both political strategy and the definition of formal organization have been discussed previously. Therefore, before concluding this chapter, it is appropriate to consider the set of policies which comprise marketing strategy.

Price Policy

Price policy involves three kinds of decisions: the fare structure, changes in the structure, and method of collection. Immediately a distinction must be made between "welfare economics" and traditional concepts of pricing. The welfare economist imputes social benefits in place of revenues, in the accounting sense, and thus is able to recommend price policies which fail to cover the full cost of service. The spectrum of welfare economics solutions ranges from maintaining a low fare, through charging no fare, to actually paying people to ride.[32]

The following interesting example of welfare economics pricing was found by the author during his field trips.[33] Inasmuch as a major trend in our urban areas is for industry to locate in the suburbs, one wonders if transit can successfully attract and profitably haul workers from their homes to suburban industrial plants. In Chicago the transit company found that an extension of a regular route to a suburban plant could not cover its costs of operation. The plant, however, entered into a subsidized service agreement which would guarantee the Transit Authority revenues of 30 passengers per trip. As of 1962 CTA was operating three morning and evening subsidized trips, carrying 133 riders, at a monthly cost to the plant of $288.50. It is interesting to speculate what the cost to the plant would be to maintain parking spaces for this number of workers. In contrast, Cleveland established special service on two routes to a suburban industrial plant using punched card data processing equipment to plan the route and schedules. It was hoped that the service would attract perhaps 400 round-trip riders to the 8,500 worker plant, but maximum daily patronage never exceeded 125. Because the service was not subsidized, Cleveland Transit had to restrict schedules to two trips per day on one route and one trip on the other. Despite heavy promotion, this lack of trips discouraged patronage. By 1962 only one round trip to the plant was being operated.

[32] For example, see the suggestion of Professor Leslie Waters in *Metropolitan Transportation*, LV (September 1959), pp. 14–20; Meyer et. al., p. 93; and Leon Moses, "Economics of Consumer Choice in Urban Transportation," *Proceedings—The Dynamics of Urban Transportation* (Detroit: Automobile Manufacturers Association, 1962), pp. 16-1–16-8.

[33] The brief descriptions of suburban plant bus service in Cleveland and Chicago and the Los Angeles "senior citizen" fare plan are summaries of case studies contained in the author's thesis.

It should also be recognized that public policy in several major cities has required a systemwide low fare structure at the risk of operating and/or capital deficits. The unfavorable 1961 operating ratios in San Francisco, New York City, and Boston (Table 2.4) can be attributed in part to this example of government pressure.

Fare Structure: In lieu of extended treatment, the author has summarized the typical types of transit fares in Table 4.5. Several of the plans will be illustrated in the remaining sections of this book.

Changes in Fares: As a rule transit companies dislike to tamper with price, not only because of community hostility, but also because of the risk of losing revenue and the increase in operating problems. A change in the fare structure means educating the public, sometimes adjusting fare boxes, delays in loading and fare collection, and increased paperwork. But as costs continue to rise, the industry has been forced to seek heavy increases in fare. Between 1920 and 1960 the average transit fare rose 280%, compared with changes in staples such as bread (+11%), butter (+7%), potatoes (+10%), and sugar (−28.4%).[34]

The industry generally accepts the validity of the Simpson & Curtin formula, which forecasts a ⅓% loss in passengers for each 1% increase in fares over a period of 3 to 12 months following the change. In terms of classical economics, this would indicate a short-run inelastic demand with a factor of .33. The formula is applied to increases in any segment of the fare structure (e.g., promotional or zone fares) to determine the loss of riders and the net effect of fare changes. Usually, after a year the secular declining trend restores revenues to their original levels, and within three years the cycle of fare increases, supported by the Simpson & Curtin formula, begins anew. Conversely, the industry views with great suspicion any decreases in fares (either systemwide or in conjunction with special promo-

---

[34] "Special Report—Fares," *Metropolitan Transportation,* LVIII (January 1962), p. 30.

Table 4.5

Types of Fare Structures: Mass Transit Industry

Type of Fare	*Discussion*
a. Flat fare	One price regardless of class of service or distance traveled.
b. Zone fare	Price increases according to distance traveled. Historically resisted by transit industry because of problems of collection.
c. Transfer charge	Evolved from free transfer privilege as costs increased, and transit companies were reluctant to increase flat or zone fares.
d. Class fare	Establishes a premium charge for special classes of service, e.g., express service.
e. Discounts	Through use of tokens, tickets, or passes a discount is offered in connection with the above types of fares.
f. Promotional	A discount fare applicable only to specific classes of riders or during certain hours of the day to promote new riding.
g. Retailer-cooperative	Attempts to promote transit and retailers by offering free rides when a specified amount of purchases are made. Not too successful.

tions) to stimulate patronage. Obviously, if demand is inelastic, revenues will decline though patronage increases.

In Chapter 3 it was noted that the segment of the population over 65 years of age is growing relative to the population in our largest cities and constitutes a major market for transit service. In early 1961 the Los Angeles Metropolitan Transit Authority instituted a reduced fare for "senior citizens." To qualify for the reduction, the rider had to secure an "ID" card. The lower fares were applicable during the hours of 10 a.m.–3 p.m. and 7 p.m.–midnight on weekdays, 7 p.m.–midnight on Saturdays, and all day Sunday. The results of this promotional fare policy provide an interesting clue as to the elasticity of demand for special segments of the riding public. Table 4.6 shows the results of the reduced fares: (a) 862,250 former peak-hour riders shifted to off peak to take advantage of the reduced fares; (b) 4,801,250 former off-peak riders continued to ride during off-peak hours,

Table 4.6

**Los Angeles Metropolitan Transit Authority: Analysis of
Senior Citizen Fare Plan, June-September 1961**

Riding Level (rides per year)

Before	8,172,750
After	10,123,000
Gain	1,950,250

Change in Riding Time (rides per year)

Riders shifted from a.m. peak to off-peak	550,250
Riders shifted from p.m. peak to off-peak	312,000
Annual rides shifted from peak to off-peak	

Financial Effects

Revenue under old plan:	8,172,750 × 22.5¢	$1,838,868
Revenue under new plan:		
Peak-hour riders	2,509,250 × 22.5¢	(564,581)
Off-peak diverted from peak	862,250 × 15¢	(129,337)
Off-peak formerly off-peak	4,801,250 × 15¢	(720,187)
Off-peak new riders	1,924,250 × 15¢	(288,638)
New Saturday riders	26,000 × 22.5¢	(5,850)
Annual *loss* in revenue from reduced fare plan		$ 130,275

At least 867,000 15¢ riders would be needed to overcome the revenue deficiency. This would mean increasing the present average rides per senior citizen per month of 17 (2 round trips per week) by 1.5 riders per month, an increase of 8.5%.

SOURCE: Los Angeles Metropolitan Transit Authority. Questionnaires were administered to 201 "senior citizens" in their homes, and the findings extrapolated to the 50,000 card holders.

(c) an additional 1,924,250 off-peak riders were attracted to the system, and (d) a small number of new Saturday riders paying full fare were attracted.

Had the Simpson and Curtin elasticity factor of .33 been applied to the 4,801,250 off-peak riders, the 33⅓% reduction in price (from 22.5 cents to 15 cents) should have produced a 10% increase in traffic (or 480,125). The revenue loss from this segment of traffic would have been $288,076. But the increase of 1,924,250 new off-peak riders added to the existing 4,801,250 generated $1,008,825 in revenue, and the revenue loss was only $71,456 (4,801,250 × 22.5 cents − 6,725,500 × 15 cents). On the other hand, the diversion of 862,250 riders from peak to off peak added an additional $64,669 (862,250 × 7.5 cents) to the annual revenue losses. These losses were offset by the $5,850 from the new full fare Saturday riders resulting in the final annual loss in revenue of $130,275 as shown in Table 4.6.

Of course, it may still be true that an increase in price would conform to the elasticity factor of .33, leading to the speculation that the demand curve may be kinked, that is, more elastic when prices are cut than when raised. But no information could be obtained to test this theory. It is perhaps more interesting to note that the basic problem was not so much the level of fares, but one of sociology. A questionnaire survey by the Authority revealed that both existing and new riders made about two round trips per week. Most of these were necessity trips, such as to a doctor. The fare cut had been designed to stimulate the number of trips made by existing riders, but the problem was that they had no place to go. The county officials are now trying to implement programs which would give senior citizens the opportunity to make more frequent trips from their homes.

In late 1961, following the elimination of tokens which increased the base fare to 25 cents, the senior citizen discount fare was raised to 20 cents. It is probable that this increase erased the net income deficit arising from the initial reduction, particularly when it is considered that the shifting of senior citizens from peak to off-peak periods might have improved bus service and reduced operating expenses.

Method of Collection: In any large city the transit company is one of the major "cash and carry" businesses. Although this reduces working capital requirements, it imposes severe problems of collection and accounting. Some companies sell tickets, tokens, and passes both as a discount-type promotional fare and to speed up service by eliminating change making. The pass has had a particularly interesting history. Under some plans the passholder was entitled to an unlimited number of rides in the hopes of stimulating off-peak riding. However, many companies hesitate to use passes today because of the possibility of abuse and the general philosophy that it gives too great a discount to persons who would ride anyway.

The problems surrounding the method of fare collection are perhaps as important and troublesome as the fare structure itself. Theoretically, an automated fare collection system, designed around a credit or validation card, would not only result in faster loading of vehicles but also yield important market research data on the characteristics of demand. The San Francisco Bay Area Rapid Transit District hopes to utilize an automated fare collection system, and as noted in Table 4–1, one Housing and Home Finance Agency Demonstration project has been designed to test automated fare collection on the Long Island Railroad.[35]

Promotion and Public Relations

This section treats these two functions together because in most transit companies the director of public relations is responsible for both public relations and promotion. It should be recognized that each can be components of marketing and/or political strategy. Promotion and public relations in the political strategy sense (measures designed to influence interest groups so as to obtain government promotion or protect against unwarranted regulation or pressure) have been discussed previously.

Public relations and promotion, in the marketing sense, can be defined as a program of keeping interest groups and the public informed as to the general health of the transit company and the services it offers. The interrelationship between public relations and promotion and the population trends discussed in Chapter 3 is extremely important. Inasmuch as the population is constantly shifting, particularly in suburban areas, it should not be assumed that the potential riding public knows even basic

[35] IRT, *Newsletter,* IV (December 15, 1963), p. 21. See also Robert S. Wilson, "Transit on Credit," *Metropolitan Transportation,* LIII (August 1957), p. 23, and Walter C. Cleave, "Mechanical Fare Collection," *Metropolitan Transportation,* LIII (December 1957), pp. 20–22.

factors about transit service, including price, routes, standards of comfort, time of trip, or vehicle headways. Furthermore, as long as the consumer is reasonably satisfied with his automobile, he probably will not make any strong efforts to find out about transit service. Only an effective continuing promotion and public relations campaign using a variety of media (press, radio, mail, speeches, etc.) can supply this information.

Thus promotion and public relations assume importance in view of transit's pressing problems of securing capital aid (political strategy) and maintaining and regaining riders (marketing strategy). Yet, the author's questionnaire (Question 7) revealed that only one of the nine respondents allocated 1% of its gross revenues to the combination of advertising and public relations. Two reported spending 0.5%, with the rest "normally budgeting" less than 0.35% of their gross revenues. By comparison, the Statistical Abstract of the United States reported that in 1960 advertising expenditures alone as a percentage of total receipts was 0.5% in the transportation industry. The comparable figure for the beverage, tobacco, chemical, and motion picture industries ranged between 4% and 5.3%.

Market Research Policy

One of the paradoxes of the urban mass transportation picture is that despite reams of statistical data, the administrators of mass transit companies, until recently, knew little about the demand for their service. At best the companies knew a great deal about patronage on a given route (peak-load point checks, on and off counts, breakdown of revenues into adult, children, tokens, etc.), but often only peak-load point counts were taken. As patronage declined, the industry found itself knowing more about its "hard core" of necessity riders, but less about those riders it lost and had to regain if it were to improve its financial position.

At the present time urban transportation studies are generating a large amount of market research type data on automobile drivers and transit riders. Hopefully, the transit industry will be able to use these data to identify different classes of riders, origins, and destinations, and design service tailored to these varied demands.

Product Planning Policy

In the author's opinion, the most important element of marketing strategy is product planning. Mass transportation is a service industry, and the attractiveness of its product can be measured by a "check list" including speed, comfort, convenience, and safety. Product planning assumes major importance, for it determines the "image" which the transit rider, and nonrider, will have of the transit company and its service. If this image is poor, no amount of pricing or promotion will lure the nonrider back (short of perhaps paying him to ride, which, as noted, is outside the scope of this study).

On the other hand, if the image of transit is one of concern for the individual rider, not simply a slow, uncomfortable gigantic production "machine," it will be far less difficult to attract riders. Therefore, the evaluation of the marketing case studies will stress heavily the appropriate place of product planning in management's strategy.

Summary

This chapter completes the overview of the industry and the introduction of a conceptual framework for identifying and analyzing environmental pressures and transit management strategies. It has been found that the future of urban mass transit rests on the ability of our central business districts and central cities to attract residents, shoppers, and industry plus the power of mass transit to divert central city and CBD triptakers from the automobile.

If the public is determined, as Dichter and others suggest, to make every trip by automobile, land use, both suburban and the central business district, will adapt itself to the automobile albeit at perhaps tremendous cost to the community. But it is far from certain whether Dichter et. al. are correct in their analysis. The 60% affirmative vote in San Francisco for an extensive rapid transit system seems to indicate that the consumer has not abandoned mass transit as he abandoned the electric interurban railway for intercity trips. Rather, the vote suggests that in our largest urban communities transit may be given one last chance to provide urban transportation which is comfortable, safe, swift, convenient, and economical.

The evidence also indicates that federal aid to transit, urban renewal, and a move toward integrating transit and highway planning have produced an external environment relatively favorable to transit, although admittedly intensifying political pressures in the process.

The analysis suggests that marketing emerges as one of the most important management strategies, notwithstanding problems of labor relations, recruitment, finance, and technology. For if management's marketing strategy can effectively use federal aid and imaginatively serve the revitalized areas of our central cities, it will create an image for transit which is one of progress, not "turn of the century" lethargy. Once the public perceives this new image of transit, it will more likely not only patronize it but support further capital improvements, and the vicious cycle of poor service, high fares, declining patronage, and poorer service may be broken. Should mass transit management fail to meet this marketing challenge, transit will become a tax-supported public service for those who cannot drive, with a status, as one official during the author's trip put it, "one step below that of the sanitation department."[36]

[36] The uncertain future of the transit industry has been noted by the aforementioned Resources for the Future, Inc., study. Their projection of local common carrier passenger volume based on the 1960 level of 9.5 billion for the years 1980 and 1990 vary from lows of 6.7 and 6.0 to highs of 15.1 and 19.2 billion respectively. Landsberg et. al., p. 649.

CHAPTER 5

Expressway Bus Service

Introduction

Perhaps the most dramatic components of our urban transportation networks to date have been the costly expressways built during the past decade. These new roads have accelerated the use of the private automobile, and siphoned off both peak and off-peak traffic from mass transit. On the other hand, several recent studies have concluded that transit can also benefit from these expressways, and suggested that in most cities express bus operation over the freeways is preferable, in terms of service and cost, to other technologies such as monorail, improved two-rail rapid transit, or rail commuter service. These studies point to the dispersal of population, lower densities of population, decentralized business districts, and movement of industry to the suburbs, which produce a diverse pattern of trip desires (in terms of space and time) that seemingly can be met only by a free-wheeling flexible vehicle such as the automobile or bus.

The Wilbur Smith study for the Automobile Manufacturers Association concludes: "In most cities, future rapid transit will take the form of express bus operations on freeways—either within specially reserved and designed peak-hour transit lanes, or along special median bus lanes."[1]

[1] Smith & Associates, p. 153. For examples of proposed bus rapid transit systems, see "Metro-Mobility, An Anatomy of a Total Bus Transit System," *Metropolitan Transportation*, LX (January 1964), pp. 11–14, and R. Gilman

The controversial Meyer, Kain, and Wohl report for the White House Panel on Civilian Technology asserts that a well-organized express bus system will almost invariably have lower costs than a rail system even at "very high volume levels."[2] The study seriously questions extensive investment in new rail systems except perhaps in cities with existing systems or having very high employment or residential densities.

The pro-rail interests within the industry have vigorously disagreed with the Meyer et. al. analysis, pointing to the fact that the labor-cost to passenger-capacity ratio of a bus is far greater than a rapid transit train.[3] In addition, they stress that the capacity of rail rapid transit in theory is three to four times that of buses, and that in fact typical rapid transit volumes are eight to twelve times expressway bus operation.[4] They imply that this ability to carry large numbers of passengers during the peak hour represents the only solution to the peak-hour load problem which would accompany a dynamic central business district. Surprisingly, in spite of this controversy, there have been almost no papers or articles published on actual expressway bus operations that go beyond descriptions of mileage, running time, equipment, or patronage, to consider questions of revenues, costs, and profitability.[5]

Smith, "Co-ordinated Transport Planning for the St. Louis Area," *Traffic Quarterly*, XIV (April 1960), pp. 143–160.

[2] Meyer et. al., p. viii.

[3] On the other hand, rail rapid transit systems incur the expenses of maintenance of way and station attendants which increase the fixed costs of operation. See Lang and Soberman, pp. 68 ff.

[4] George Anderson, "Rail and Bus Rapid Transit for Downtown Access," *Proceedings—The Dynamics of Urban Transportation* (Detroit: Automobile Manufacturers Association, 1962), pp. 7-12–7-15. Theoretical expressway bus capacity (25% standees) is 15,000 persons per hour versus rail rapid transit's 48,000–72,000. Observed volumes outside of New York City were: bus, 803–5,595 per hour, and rapid transit 6,211–10,376 per hour. Within the New York City area counts disclosed: bus, 23,187 on approaches to Port Authority Bus Terminal during one hour, and rail transit 62,000 persons per hour.

[5] See Wolfgang S. Homburger and Norman Kennedy, *The Utilization of Freeways by Urban Transit Buses: A Nationwide Survey* (Berkeley: University of California Institute of Transportation and Traffic Engineering, 1958). The aforementioned HHFA experiments (Chapter 4) should also add to the

An excellent exception was a 1956 study by Wolfgang Homburger of express bus operations in San Francisco. His analysis, which avoided the pitfall of average costs, concluded that at the historically low flat fare in San Francisco, the new services, though popular, could not cover out-of-pocket costs.[6]

This chapter will report four case studies of expressway bus operations in Los Angeles, Chicago, Cleveland, and Philadelphia. The cases include data on daily and peak-hour patronage, average speeds, and profitability, but, more important, will give a better understanding of the marketing strengths and weaknesses of today's transit management. Chapter 6 will follow with the presentation of four case studies of investments in rail rapid transit. To avoid needless repetition, some of the analysis (such as the absence of air conditioning), which could well be included in Chapter 5, will be deferred until Chapter 6.

Los Angeles Metropolitan Transit Authority: The West Valley Freeway Flyer

Shortly after it became an operating agency, the Los Angeles Metropolitan Transit Authority (LAMTA)[7] inaugurated Route #35, the West Valley Freeway Flyer, an expressway bus service connecting the Los Angeles central business district with Reseda, via Tarzana, Encino, Studio City, and the Hollywood Freeway (Map).

---

literature on express bus operations. In particular the results of an HHFA demonstration grant to St. Louis' Bi-State Transportation Agency, approved in February 1964, will be of interest. The project involves the establishment of seven new air-conditioned express bus routes between the suburbs and the central business district. Several of the routes use St. Louis' growing expressway system. For details see *Passenger Transport,* February 28, 1964, p. 1.

[6] Wolfgang Homburger, *A Study of Express Bus Operation on Freeways* (Berkeley: University of California Institute of Transportation and Traffic Engineering, 1956).

[7] See Kennedy and Homburger, *Organization of Metropolitan Transit Agencies,* for a concise history of the LAMTA. As of the fall of 1964, it was anticipated that the Los Angeles Metropolitan Transit Authority would soon be absorbed by the newly created Southern California Rapid Transit District.

Los Angeles Metropolitan Transit Authority: West Valley Freeway Flyer Service, July 1962

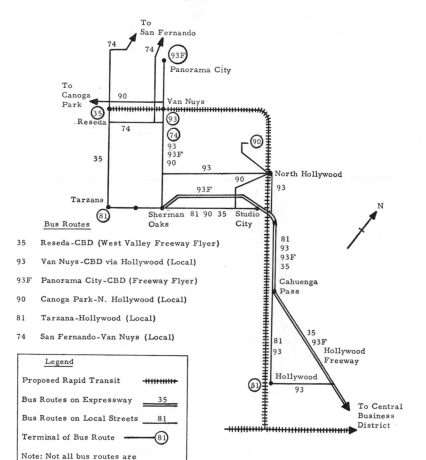

To
San Fernando

74
74
93F
Panorama City

To
Canoga
Park
90
Van Nuys
35
.Reseda
74
93
74
93
93F
90
35
93
Tarzana
93F
81
North Hollywood
90
93
90
Sherman 81 90 35 Studio
Oaks City

81
93
93F
35
Cahuenga
Pass

35
81 93F
93 Hollywood
Freeway

Hollywood
81
93

N

To Central
Business
District

Bus Routes

35   Reseda-CBD (West Valley Freeway Flyer)

93   Van Nuys-CBD via Hollywood (Local)

93F   Panorama City-CBD (Freeway Flyer)

90   Canoga Park-N. Hollywood (Local)

81   Tarzana-Hollywood (Local)

74   San Fernando-Van Nuys (Local)

Legend

Proposed Rapid Transit	+++++++++
Bus Routes on Expressway	35
Bus Routes on Local Streets	81
Terminal of Bus Route	—(81)

Note: Not all bus routes are
shown nor is map
drawn to scale

Historically, this western section of the San Fernando Valley had been served by a Pacific Electric interurban rail line between Canoga Park, San Fernando, Van Nuys, and Los Angeles. In 1938 rail service to Canoga Park and San Fernando was replaced by shuttle bus service to Van Nuys. In 1952 the remaining rail route was abandoned in favor of Route #93, which offered local and express bus service from Van Nuys to the CBD via Hollywood.[8] The growing towns of Studio City, Sherman Oaks, Encino, Tarzana, and Reseda still were not given direct bus service to downtown Los Angeles until the establishment of Route #35.

The new line operated in the peak direction only during the rush hours, carried no local passengers, and featured a "seats-for-all" loading standard policy. The service was heavily promoted, including the distribution of 25,000 free timetables in the service area.

Weekly patronage (5 days) climbed from 1,341 during the first month (August 1958) to a peak of 5,940 riders in 1960. The initial schedule of 4 daily round trips was increased to 14. Patronage declined slightly by 1962, but the 14 trips remained.

A postcard survey taken by LAMTA personnel in 1960 revealed that 60% of the riders formerly used their automobile for the trip, and that 47% of the riders reached the bus route by automobile (either dropped off or parked). The survey also showed that traffic congestion on the expressway made it impossible to adhere to schedules consistently, and that therefore few riders used LAMTA feeder buses to reach the new route.

The success of Route #35 ultimately resulted in a complete revamping of the San Fernando Valley service in late 1962. The Freeway Flyer service was expanded, and new routes were instituted to better serve the public.

---

[8] For a history of the Pacific Electric interurban rail line in the San Fernando Valley see Hilton and Due, *The Electric Interurban Railways in America*, p. 413. Bus Route #93 used the Hollywood Freeway between the central business district and Santa Monica Boulevard (4.4 miles) en route to Hollywood, but except for a short freeway section over Cahuenga Pass it stayed on local streets for the remainder of its run. However, a few rush-hour trips bypassed Hollywood and stayed on the Freeway for nine miles.

At the present time, LAMTA is pressing hard for a rail rapid transit system. One route would connect North Hollywood with the central business district. If the route should ever be built, the wheel will have come the full circle, for the bus service from the West Valley will undoubtedly again begin feeding a rail line, rather than operating directly to the central business district.

Chicago Transit Authority:
Express Bus Service on the Northwest Expressway

In the winter of 1960 the Chicago Transit Authority (CTA) began operation of Route #19, the Devon-Northwest Express, a rush-hour-only bus service connecting the northwest section of the city with the Milwaukee Avenue rapid transit terminal at Logan Square via the $237 million Northwest Expressway (Map).

CTA had been successful in obtaining space in the median strip of the expressway for an extension of the Milwaukee Avenue rapid transit line, in the same manner as its celebrated Congress median strip rapid transit line (Chapter 6). But the Authority was unable to obtain financing for the $31 million project. Opposition included the Chicago & North Western Railroad,[9] the state legislature, the American Automobile Association,[10] and even one segment of the academic community.[11] Therefore, when the expressway opened, it established Route #19 to produce a "riding habit" pending the future extension of rapid transit, as well as to show both residents and other transit operators in the CTA service area that it was ready, willing, and able to provide new services to meet the needs of the community.

[9] The C&NW stressed that the rapid transit line would divert rail commuters as well as automobile drivers. See Chapter 3, note 31, for a description of C&NW's investment in commuter equipment.

[10] The position of the AAA as well as many in the state legislature was that CTA was established as an autonomous transit authority with no taxing power. The $31 million rapid transit extension was a part of a $315 million package proposed by CTA, which would be financed by a combination of CTA revenues, motor fuel taxes, and real estate taxes. CTA's position was that transit riders should finance "above-the-rail costs," but that taxes should be used to cover the costs of right-of-way.

[11] A research study at Northwestern University commented on the $315

Chicago Transit Authority:
Express Bus Routes on the Northwest Expressway

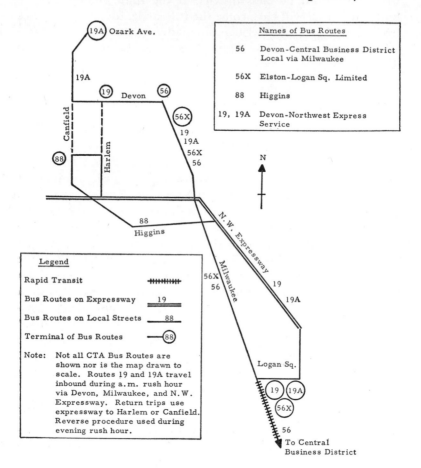

million package (including the Northwest Expressway line) as follows: ". . . it should suffice to say that the Authority, however competent it is to operate a bus and transit service, does not have the competence or authorization to assess or prescribe community benefits or needs, and that technical efficiencies in a free society count for far less than individual choice." Northwestern University Transportation Center, *Basic Issues in Chicago Metropolitan Transportation* (Chicago: Northwestern, 1958), p. 24.

Following the increase in daily riders from 1,600 to 2,500 during the first year of operation, CTA extended the route one mile into a new service area (Route 19A on map). It rejected, however, a staff proposal to inaugurate a similar bus service which would have branched off the expressway to follow the existing Route #88 line.

The increase in patronage from the one-mile extension was offset by a systemwide transfer charge, which raised the price of a combination bus-rapid transit trip by 5 cents. In mid-1962 the line carried 2,500 riders daily. Total vehicle trips (both directions) increased from 32 daily in 1960 to 45 by 1962.

Towards the end of 1962 both the Chicago Area Transportation Study and an independent engineering firm recommended that the rail rapid transit line in the Northwest Expressway be built as planned. At the present time there appears to be a good possibility that the Devon-Northwest Express, having served its purpose as a transition between a period of no service and rail rapid transit, will pass out of existence during the next decade.[12]

Cleveland Transit System:
Extension of an Expressway Bus Route

On July 17, 1961, following a favorable feasibility study, the Cleveland Transit System (CTS) extended service on one of its heaviest routes (#55-Clifton) six miles to serve the town of Bay Village. The new service (#55-C) was 17.5 miles long, and utilized the Memorial Shoreway nonstop for three miles (Map). The extension had been requested by the mayor of Bay Village, whose town was then being served by another suburban bus line.

The plan of operation featured direct bus service to the central business district, rather than a feeder operation to the

---

[12] It should be noted that during 1963 CTA inaugurated two more new bus lines using the South Expressway. CTA hopes to extend its rapid transit lines in the median strip of this expressway in the same manner as on the Northwest Expressway. Again, CTA may be said to have used express buses as a transition service pending rapid transit extensions. See *Passenger Transport*, December 6, 1963, p. 6.

Cleveland Transit System:
Rapid Transit System and Bay Village Bus Service

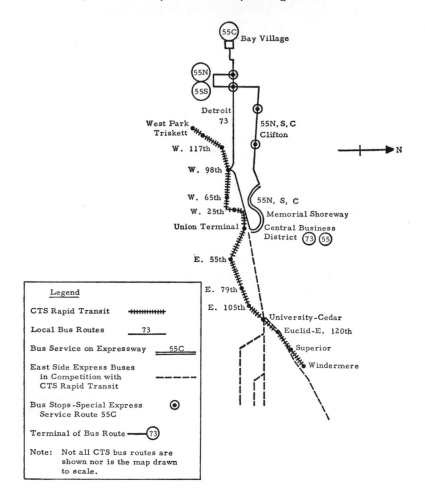

rapid transit system at West 98th-Detroit station; limited stop express trips during the peak hours; complete day and evening service; a fare schedule tailored to the length of the route; and a seats-for-all loading policy. Promotion included the passing out of 4,300 pamphlets door to door and the periodic mailing of timetables to those who requested them.

The extension immediately began to cover its costs of operation and was soon viewed as a routine operation by CTA officials. The 1961 Annual Report concluded: "Acceptance of [this] service by our riders gave proof that people can be attracted to safe, dependable, rapid transportation."

Philadelphia Transportation Company: Expressway Bus Service to Ardmore

In February 1962, following approval of the State's Public Utilities Commission over the vigorous protests of the Pennsylvania Railroad, the Philadelphia Transportation Company extended an existing expressway bus service from the city limits of Philadelphia to Ardmore, Pennsylvania[13] (Map). Inasmuch as the territory between Ardmore and City Avenue was then being served by the suburban Red Arrow Lines, PTC entered into a unique agreement with Red Arrow, whereby each would supply 50% of the equipment for the new direct service between Ardmore and the Philadelphia CBD.

In contrast to the rush-hour-only service which had existed on the PTC route which was being extended, the Ardmore Express (designated as Route #44) operated throughout the day and on evenings when stores were open. Trips were scheduled so as to provide seats-for-all, and the fare for the full trip was the total of the PTC and Red Arrow local charges.

[13] The existing route operated from 54th Street and City Avenue to City Hall in downtown Philadelphia via the expressway. The extended line used an existing Red Arrow suburban bus route to Ardmore on one end, and a longer downtown loop on the other. The extended downtown loop provided direct service to major department stores at 8th and Market. The effect of the new line was to eliminate transfers and provide one bus service for the first time between Ardmore and downtown Philadelphia.

Philadelphia Transportation Company:
Market-Frankford Rapid Transit
and Ardmore Express Bus Service

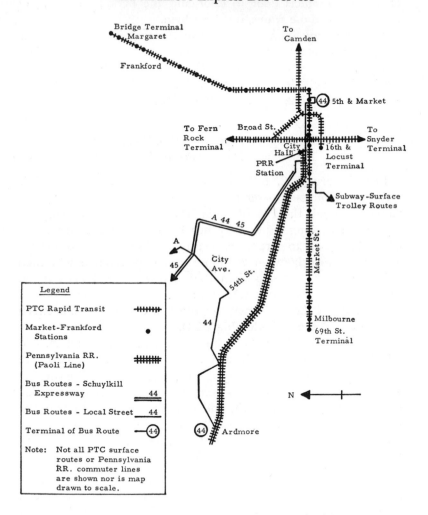

Within three months patronage reached the anticipated 2,400 daily passengers, and by October 1962 had climbed to over 3,100 daily riders. Most of the growth took place within PTC territory. The success of the Ardmore express prompted PTC to begin another expressway bus route in the summer of 1962, making a total of three PTC express bus lines using the Schuylkill Expressway for an appreciable length.

Patronage and Profitability of Expressway Bus Routes

Patronage

A comparative analysis of patronage statistics is set forth in Table 5.1. The most apparent characteristic of each of the study routes is their relatively low volume of patronage. For example, during the peak rush hour, three of the four lines carried between 320 and 400 riders, less than the typical load of a single rapid transit train. Only Chicago's Devon-Northwest Express handled appreciable numbers of riders, but even its 1962 peak-hour volume was not much greater than 1,000 riders.

It should be noted, however, that the routes in Cleveland, Philadelphia, and Los Angeles operated on the expressways together with other bus lines. In Cleveland, Route #55C shared the Memorial Shoreway with two other routes and the combined weekday patronage in 1961 was 15,566 riders. In Philadelphia the weekday patronage on the Schuylkill expressway Routes A and #44 (see map) before the inauguration of Route #45 in 1962 was 8,000 riders. The West Valley Freeway Flyer in Los Angeles was one of four lines to use the Hollywood Freeway, and checks during 1962 showed 3,798 weekday riders. As will be seen in the following chapter, these aggregate expressway bus patronage totals were substantially less than rail rapid transit volumes.

Because of this low-volume operation, increases in express bus patronage are frequently reported in terms of dramatically high percentage changes. It is interesting to note that the oldest routes studied (Los Angeles and Chicago) passed through a stage of

Table 5.1

Patronage:
Expressway Bus Routes

Nature of Statistic	Los Angeles (LAMTA)	Chicago (CTA)	Cleveland (CTS)	Philadelphia (PTC)
Typical patronage per weekday	1,132[1]	2,541[2]	1,329[3]	3,193[4]
Initial % change weekday riders	9/58–9/60 +181%	12/60–4/61 +46%	—	3/62–6/62 +28%
More recent % change, weekday riders	9/60–6/62 −5%	4/61–4/62 +4%	7/61–2/63 +45%	6/62–10/62 +34%
Recent patronage, peak direction, peak-hour–weekday	386[5] (1962)	812[6] (1962)	364[7] (1963)	322[8] (1962)
Percent persons formerly used automobile	60%	No Survey Taken	No Survey Taken	No Survey Taken

[1] Operated weekdays only between hours of 6:10–9:30 a.m. and 2:50–6:10 p.m. Check taken in June 1962. No reverse service.

[2] Operated weekdays only between hours of 6:23–8:23 a.m. and 4:20–6:20 p.m., but carried passengers in reverse direction. Check taken in April 1962.

[3] Operated weekdays and Saturdays. Weekday service offered between 5:54 a.m. and 11:50 p.m. Check of riders, February 1963, was made between hours of 6:03–9:54 a.m. and 2:54–6:25 p.m. at the peak-load point. Therefore, total weekday patronage may have been as high as 1,600 daily riders, for a total of 31 bus trips was not checked.

[4] Operated weekdays and Saturdays. Weekday service offered between 6:20 a.m.–6:35 p.m. (9:15 p.m. on Wednesday evenings). Check made in October 1962.

[5] Estimated by author; 568 persons carried between 2:50–6:10 p.m. Peak-hour factor based on similar Cleveland data.

[6] Based on average load during two-hour period applied to the 14 trips during peak hour. Actual peak load undoubtedly higher, although it cannot be determined from data.

[7] Based on actual count of 8 westbound trips during peak hour.

[8] Based on average peak load during peak hour (reported to author as 46 westbound) applied to the 7 westbound trips during the peak hour.

initial growth and then experienced either a decline or a sub, stantially smaller growth pattern. On the other hand, in 1962 both Cleveland and Philadelphia were still in the initial stages of high percentage growth, although neither carried a high volume of rush-hour riders.

In short, each of the study routes operated on a very small scale. Equipment requirements ranged from 8 to 14 buses, involving at the most a capital investment of less than $450,000.

Profitability

In theory, it should be relatively easy to determine the profitability of a bus route, for the problem encountered in rapid transit of costing labor and other expenses for trains of different lengths is avoided. Unfortunately, though, it is difficult to determine with accuracy a route's profitability because of questions of the allocation of overhead and the assignment of revenues. The relationship between the major elements of operating expenses (excluding depreciation and fixed charges) is shown in Table 5.2, taken from the income statement of one of the study companies' bus operations.

It is obvious from the tabulation that the minimum out-of-pocket costs (direct labor and expenses associated with direct labor, such as social security, maintenance, and fuel) constitute the majority (about 72%) of the total operating expenses (excluding depreciation and fixed charges). In turn, labor and expenses directly related to labor make up the majority of the minimum out-of-pocket costs. Although the direct labor component of the total costs can be costed accurately by noting the total hours for each route on the schedule sheets, the remaining costs must be allocated by mileage, or some other factor, and thus are subject to the inaccuracies imposed by using systemwide averages for a particular route.

The problem of allocation of revenues hinges on either the use of a vehicle on different routes during the day or the amount of transfer passengers on a given bus line. For example, some companies operate buses with locked fareboxes on different lines each day, making it impossible to allocate revenues to the

Table 5.2

**Operating Expense Statement:
Bus Operations**

Account	*Varies With*	*Percentage of Operating Expenses*
Way and Structures	Allocated-Mileage	2.3%
Maintenance-Equipment	Allocated-Mileage	18.6
Power-Fuel	Allocated-Mileage	3.5
Transportation: Direct Labor	Hours	47.2
Other Labor & Materials*	Allocated-Mileage	6.4
General Expenses Directly Related to Operation†	Allocated-Mileage Hours, and % Revenues	17.8
General & Administrative (Traffic)	Allocated-Mileage	4.2
Total Operating Expenses	(Excluding Depreciation and Interest)	100.0%

* Includes superintendence, etc.

† This company includes injuries and damages (function of revenues), group insurance, and social security (percentage of direct labor), pensions (allocated-mileage), and rental of leased lines and facilities (allocated-mileage) in this category.

separate routes. In other cases, a line may carry many transfer passengers, yet its revenues will be low.

Some companies take the annual revenue for each line, divide it by the vehicle miles, and compare the result to the system average operating expenses per vehicle mile to obtain a measure of profitability. This procedure can lead to extremely inaccurate results for express bus operation. For example, Chicago's Devon-Northwest Express grossed 29.98 cents per mile in 1961, versus a systemwide vehicle operating cost (excluding administrative and depreciation) of 72.28 cents per bus mile. During the year 183,570 miles were operated, and thus it would appear that the line "lost" $79,302. But because the line operated at average speeds nearly double the system average, the same labor costs produced more vehicle miles; thus its average cost per mile of operation was substantially less than that of the system.

Transit also faces the problem of fixed and variable costs, in that when a man shows up for work, he must be paid a full day's wage, even though he makes only a few trips. Thus the incremental costs for off-peak service may amount to only the mileage charges for maintenance fuel and tires.

In short, because of the complexities of the labor contracts, the nature of the accounting systems, and the difficulties in assigning revenues, it is not always easy to determine the profitability of a given bus route. The author attempted, however, to find out if the four routes in question covered both minimum out-of-pocket costs and total operating expenses (excluding depreciation and fixed charges). The author has concluded from the data supplied to him (Table 5.3) that:

(1) In 1961–1962 the revenue on the long suburban-Central Business District routes in Philadelphia, Cleveland, and Los Angeles definitely covered minimum operating expenses and allocated overhead, and in Philadelphia it also covered depreciation and fixed charges.

(2) In 1961 Chicago's Devon-Northwest Express probably covered its minimum out-of-pocket costs (labor, maintenance, fuel), but its revenues exceeded total operating expenses (excluding depreciation and fixed charges) only if a relatively high proportion of its riders were new to CTA.[14]

On the other hand, none of the routes could be termed a "heavy profit maker."[15] Profitability depends largely on factors that will be discussed in the remainder of this chapter under the headings of marketing strategy, political strategy, and formal organization.

[14] In early February 1961 the CTA schedule department took passenger counts on Routes #19, #56, and #56X (Map). Of the 2,139 passengers on Route #19, 719 were assumed to have been diverted from Routes #56 and #56X. This was a much smaller number of diversions than had been anticipated. On the other hand, no survey was made of actual riders on Route #19 to find previous modes of transportation; therefore the 1,400 figure assumes that the only CTA diversions were from Routes #56 and #56X.

[15] The questionnaire (Question 9) found that only four of nine respondents believed expressway buses could cover all costs.

Table 5.3

Profitability:
Expressway Bus Routes, Study Cities

1. *Los Angeles: West Valley Freeway Flyer*

   As of July 1962 the route grossed approximately $650 per day. The ratio of revenue to minimum out-of-pocket costs (labor, fuel, and maintenance) was 1.20. If depreciation and insurance were added, the ratio dropped to 1.06. If depreciation was excluded, but replaced by other elements of direct and indirect overhead (e.g. pensions), the revenues appeared to cover total operating expenses (excluding depreciation and fixed charges).

2. *Chicago: Devon-Northwest Express*

   Annual 1961 revenues varied from $55,000 to $110,000 depending on the following allocations: (a) $110,060—100% revenues paid by round-trip riders allocated to bus route. (b) $73,000—66% round-trip revenues allocated to bus and 34% to rapid transit based on proportion of total route mileage between Ozark and Central Business District accounted for by each. (c) $55,030—50% of round-trip revenues allocated to bus route. (d) $91,900—Assumes 1,420 of the 2,139 daily round-trip riders were new to CTA as estimated by the CTA schedule department. Out-of-pocket costs in 1961 (direct labor, fuel, tires, and maintenance) were $70,747 for the bus route. General and administrative expenses on the basis of mileage were about $5,700. Thus, if the 1,400 new rider estimate was accurate, the route covered total operating expenses (excluding depreciation and fixed charges).

3. *Cleveland: Bay Village Express Service*

   Original breakeven analysis indicated that 750 daily riders would be needed to meet total operating expenses (excluding depreciation, fixed charges, and certain taxes). As of 1962 the line carried over 1,300 daily riders and CTS officials stated it was "paying its way."

4. *Philadelphia: Ardmore Express Route #44*

   Original calculations showed that if 2,400 daily riders were carried, the revenues would cover wages (including benefits and payroll taxes), fuel, maintenance, tires, claims, and depreciation. As of October 1962 the route carried 3,193 daily riders, and the revenue of $7.01 per working hour covered "all out-of-pocket expenses plus depreciation and allocated overhead costs."

SOURCES: Company data and interviews.

Marketing Strategy

Price Policy

Testimony to the diversity of thought within the transit industry concerning appropriate pricing policies is given in the finding that each company being studied priced its expressway bus service in a different manner.

Los Angeles applied its system zone fare to Route #35, but made no effort to charge a premium fare for the express service. On the other hand, Chicago, in keeping with its "one city—one fare policy," charged the local bus fare of 25 cents, even though over half the route was nonstop and the distance from the rapid transit to the outer terminal was over 9 miles. Cleveland, consistent with its system policy of charging a differential fare for a premium service (express bus or rapid transit), built up the fare from the local rate plus a 5-cent premium, but because of the extraordinary length of the route also added a zone charge of 15 cents.

Philadelphia, like Chicago, charged only the local fare of 23 cents for the portion of its route within PTC territory, but in view of the length of the route and the joint service with the Red Arrow lines, the through rider between Red Arrow territory and the CBD paid a combination PTC-Red Arrow fare, as if he had transferred from one company to the other during the trip. In effect, this produced a zone fare, similar to Los Angeles.

Table 5.4 shows the effect of these different approaches to pricing policy. The rate per mile varies from 2.69 cents (actually 2.13 cents for the combination bus-rapid transit trip) on CTA's Devon-Northwest Express to 3.74 cents under the Los Angeles zone fare structure.

One of the most interesting aspects of expressway bus marketing strategy was the interrelationship between pricing and product planning in determining the profitability of the service. Succeeding sections of this chapter will focus on price versus standards of comfort and price versus nonstop express service.

Table 5.4

Rates of Fare:
Expressway Bus Service, Study Cities

Nature of *Statistic*	*Los Angeles* *(LAMTA)*	*Chicago* *(CTA)*	*Cleveland* *(CTS)*	*Philadelphia* *(PTC)*
Fare to outer terminal	89¢[1]	25¢[2]	45¢	46¢
Rate per mile to outer terminal	3.74¢	2.69¢[3]	2.57¢	3.29¢

[1] Included federal tax of 8 cents abolished in 1963.

[2] Did not include 5-cent transfer charge to rapid transit at Logan Square Station for remaining 4.8-mile trip to CBD.

[3] The rate per mile for the combined bus-rapid transit trip (14.1 miles) was 2.13 cents.

Market Research Policy

Market research is defined as the systematic effort to learn about the potential and actual demand for urban mass transit. The express bus cases demonstrate both strengths and weaknesses in the marketing research efforts.

Because of the relatively small scale of the operation, several companies were able to estimate rather accurately the demand for bus service. Both Philadelphia (possibly for regulatory purposes as well as determining the feasibility of the service) and Chicago made a count of the households within the "service area" of the route. The "service area" was defined in terms of distance of the homes from the streets served by the bus line. In Chicago's case the estimate was further refined by the number of persons expected to be diverted from paralleling local and express services.

In contrast to rapid transit feasibility studies, no attempts were made to forecast patronage from those outside the "normal" service area, that is, those who might drive to the bus lines. None of the bus routes terminated at parking lots, and it is reasonable to assume that the forecasters did not believe there would be many combination automobile-bus patrons. In this respect, it is quite significant to note that the one postcard survey made on any of the four routes (Los Angeles) showed that 47% of the patrons either drove and parked along the bus route or were dropped off at bus stops by automobile. By simply counting the households in the "service area," the potential patronage may be seriously underestimated, and if subsequent promotion is directed only to those who can walk to the bus (instead of both park-ride and "service area" patrons), the forecast may turn into a "self-fulfilling prophecy."

In the author's opinion, another defect in the market research effort was the failure to probe deeper into the nature of the riders. Only Los Angeles, as mentioned, made a postcard survey, which yielded information on former mode of transport, purpose of trip, and method of reaching the route, and in turn led to further improvements in service.

The question of former mode of transportation is particularly important in the case of express buses. If riders are simply diverted from other routes, the incremental revenues to the system may not cover incremental costs. The only time when such intrasystem diversions are beneficial is when a bus can be removed from local service following the diversion of riders to faster express service, for the faster speeds permit better utilization of labor.

Promotion Policy

In each of the cases, the author felt that in view of the budget constraints the promotion was good. Each of the companies made extensive use of pamphlets and timetables, as well as the traditional press releases, to announce the new routes. Several of the companies employed women "sales representatives" to hand out descriptive literature at homes being served for the first time. Los Angeles literally blitzed the service area, with over 25,000 timetables being distributed. Cleveland's policy of mailing seasonally timetables to over 100,000 homes was an outstanding example of personalized selling. Its 1958 budget for timetables and mailing for the whole system was only $27,700.

In the author's opinion, this was a quite reasonable sum to spend for a company grossing over $27 million.

The timetables were informative and easy to read. Each trip's time of arrival and departure from major intersections was clearly indicated. Some timetables also contained helpful supplemental information including the map of the route, transfer points, and the fare structures.

Some officials in the transit industry feel that timetables are a nuisance and/or wasteful. They argue that the schedules are always changing, the buses do not run on time, or headways are so close that no timetable is needed. Yet, each of these reasons can be cited in a justification for timetables. If the schedules change, that is all the more reason to inform the public. If the buses do not run on time, the rider can be the most effective supervisor by informing the company that certain trips are consistently off schedule. The company can then check the running time and make adjustments. Finally, if the headways are close together, the timetables will spotlight this excellent service. And even though headways may be close, a person may choose to drive simply because he does not know how long the transit trip will take.

It is indisputable that one of the major attractions of the private automobile to the urban traveler is its immediate availability. Timetables, properly distributed, permit planning by the potential rider, and can thus bring to mass transit the standards of convenience inherent in the automobile.

Promotion can be used not only to inform actual transit riders, but as an important component in transit's public relations program, aimed at riders and nonriders alike. This second aspect of promotion will be considered in the following chapter in connection with rail rapid transit.

Product Planning Policy

In Chapter 4 product planning was defined as those decisions concerning speed, comfort, convenience, and safety which can enhance the transit "product." Although transit's excellent safety record, when compared to its competitor the automobile, cannot be challenged, the other elements require some examination.

Comfort: It is obvious, at least to this author, that one of the major attractions of the automobile is its comfort. Even when the driver is fighting traffic, he does so in privacy, on an upholstered seat, listening to the radio, smoking a cigarette. In contrast, the usual picture of transit bus operations during the rush hour is one of a rolling sardine box with "always room for one more, and please step to the rear of the bus." Yet, three of the routes studied (Los Angeles, Philadelphia, and Cleveland) illustrate dramatic reversals of this traditional rush-hour policy. Table 5.5 indicates that during the rush hour, headways were constructed so that in most cases there was a seat for every rider on the three routes.

It must be admitted that in each of the cases there were still some standees on one or two of the rush-hour trips, for there is generally a peak fifteen minutes within the peak hour. Yet the

Table 5.5

Comparative Standards of Comfort:
Rush-Hour Expressway Buses, Study Cities

Nature of Statistic	Los Angeles (LAMTA)	Chicago (CTA)	Cleveland (CTS)	Philadelphia (PTC)
Seated capacity per vehicle	50	50	52	47
Standees per vehicle	25	25	26	24
Trips per peak hour, peak direction	8	14	8	7
Seats per peak hour, peak direction	400	700	416	329
Seated and standing capacity, peak hour	600	1,050	624	497
Reported peak loads	386[1]	812[2]	364	322
Per cent peak loads to total seats available	96.5%	116%	87.5%	98%

[1] Estimated by author. See Table 5.1.

[2] Based on average load over 2-hour period. Peak load during peak hour undoubtedly higher, thus increasing the percentage of total load/total seats available.

importance of the statistics lies in the fact that the transit managements tried to lure long distance riders on expressway buses
by recognizing the need of providing the basic element of comfort
guaranteed by the automobile—the seat.

It is important to note that a higher fare had to be charged to
offset the seats-for-all policy, if the bus service was to be profitable.
Unlike rapid transit, where two men can operate a train with as
many as 500 seats, bus operation requires an expensive driver for
each 50 seats. Cleveland's Bay Village premium fare enabled the
route to cover its costs while hauling seated loads. On the other
hand, Chicago's flat fare made it difficult for the Devon-Northwest Express to cover its total operating costs after allocating a
share of the revenues to the connecting rapid transit line, even
though the bus route carried standing loads.

Speed: Many express bus advocates emphasize the dual ability of a bus to circulate through a suburban "pick-up" area and
then drive at high speeds over the expressway network to the
CBD. In each of the study cases, the buses operate in the above
manner. Unfortunately the end product is a classic example of
the saying that "you can't have your cake and eat it too." For
the pick-up operation is extremely time-consuming and lowers
the average speed of the journey. In addition, rush-hour congestion on the expressways sometimes prevents the buses from attain-
ing their maximum speed. (Proponents of bus operation hope
for separate lanes, but as yet none have been constructed, for
political and economic reasons.) Table 5.6 thus shows that the
average terminal-to-terminal speed fell within a range of 14 to 20
mph during the peak periods, certainly better than many local
routes, but clearly inferior to the average speeds of an automobile.

Shortly after the author's visit Los Angeles reversed its policy
on the West Valley Freeway Flyer. Initially, the route handled
no local riders and its pick-up zone constituted less than half the
route.[16] In 1962, however, the line was extended an additional

16 The West Valley Freeway Flyer initially picked up passengers between
Reseda and Studio City inbound. One inbound stop was made to discharge
passengers at a bus turnout along the Hollywood Freeway. This policy of
handling no local riders emphasized the suburbia-CBD commuter orientation
of the route and minimized the problems of fare collection under the

Table 5.6

Comparative Standards of Speed:
Rush-Hour Expressway Buses, Study Cities

Nature of Statistic	Los Angeles (LAMTA)	Chicago (CTA)	Cleveland (CTS)	Philadelphia (PTC)
Length of bus route (miles)	23.8	9.3[1]	17.5	14.0
Running time peak-hour–range in minutes[2]	75–79	37–39	54–62	51–54
Average speed peak-hour–range in mph	18.1–19.0	14.3–15.1	16.9–19.4	15.6–16.5

[1] CTA's Devon-Northwest Express did not directly serve the CBD. Passengers transferred to the rapid transit line at Logan Square. The rapid transit running time added about 15 minutes to the trip for the additional 4.8 miles.

[2] Times shown were for *outbound* trips during the peak hour. Inbound times were usually slightly faster. During other segments of the 4-hour rush-hour period (7–9 a.m., 4–6 p.m.), when traffic conditions were less crowded, times were substantially better; e.g., LAMTA 64 minutes; CTA 35 minutes; CTS 54 is best time; and PTC 46 minutes.

7 miles to split terminals, and now permits local riding over the outer 8 miles of the route. Although this extended pick-up zone was designed to improve service and increase revenues, it remains to be seen whether this slower service will attract substantial numbers of riders.

The expressway bus operations in Chicago and Philadelphia have yielded evidence that extending the local pick-up zone may not attract substantial numbers of riders. Chicago's one-mile extension of its Devon-Northwest service carried only 180 daily riders (of a total of 2,541 daily) in both directions. In Philadelphia a check taken in October 1962, after five months of operation, found that only 462 round-trip CBD-oriented riders boarded in the outer half of the Ardmore Express route (the extension of

---

LAMTA zone fare system. But it prohibited passenger turnover en route (i.e., a local passenger replacing another), thus placing a relatively low revenue limit on each trip.

an existing PTC expressway route) compared to 2,023 originating in PTC territory. Of course, much of the reduced level of riding in the outer end can be attributed to the lower density of population. It also seems reasonable to assume that the higher average speeds available to the rider who lives closest to the nonstop expressway portion of the route are persuasive in attracting patronage.

As in the case of the seats-for-all policy, the use of express service to increase product quality requires a trade-off with pricing for profitable operation. Inasmuch as the nonstop portion of the route prohibits passenger turnover en route, a relatively higher fare must be charged over local service to generate acceptable levels of revenue per hour or vehicle mile.

The ability of the bus to offer express service to any portion of the city has another advantage besides speed. This flexibility permits segregation of long-haul from short-haul traffic. This subject will be examined more closely in the following chapter.

Convenience—Nature of Route and Hours of Service: It is interesting to compare the various policies on the nature of the route as illustrated in these four cases. An important feature of both the Philadelphia and Los Angeles services was that each gave the outer terminal a direct central business district bus route for the first time.

In the planning stage of Chicago's Devon-Northwest line, the major question was whether the route should feed the rapid transit at Logan Square (as did the existing Milwaukee Avenue Limited—Route #56X on map) or operate directly to the central business district via the expressway. The transportation department strongly opposed direct service because of rush-hour congestion on the expressway and a policy of supporting, rather than competing with, the rapid transit system. It believed that the excellent CBD distribution and frequency of service on the rapid transit line would offset the disadvantage of transferring. The general manager supported this position, and the service was operated as a feeder to the rapid transit. This decision permitted half of the buses to double back to the outer terminal each rush hour to make a second trip, thus increasing the productivity of the drivers and vehicles and offsetting the disadvantage of the low flat fare discussed previously. On the other hand, Cleveland's management had the opportunity to operate its Bay Village express bus as a feeder to the rapid transit system at the W. 98th Street station (following Route #73), but preferred to route the buses directly to the CBD in competition with the Rapid. In short, transit managements in Chicago, Cleveland, and Philadelphia had to weigh the possible advantages of cost and perhaps time savings from feeder service to rapid transit lines against the undeniable convenience of direct one-vehicle service to the CBD.

Another important decision which determined the character and patronage of the new routes was the hours of service. The expressway bus routes in Chicago and Los Angeles operated during the rush hours only, probably to avoid the possibility of out-of-pocket losses from overextended service, yet handle the peak demand. On the other hand, both Cleveland and Philadelphia offered a much more complete daytime service, as well as trips on Saturday and during evenings when the stores were open, and both routes succeeded in contributing to depreciation and fixed charges.

It is ironic that the "transition" expressway routes in Chicago and Los Angeles (in the sense that it was hoped they would be succeeded by rail rapid transit) provided the minimum service in contrast to the "permanent" routes in Cleveland and Philadelphia. In terms of public and political relations, complete service would seem a major asset in developing grass roots support for the transit company, and in turn might lead to the approval of rapid transit lines. Yet, because of the cost considerations, both Los Angeles and Chicago declined to make an investment in full service designed to attract shopping and recreational as well as work trips. Los Angeles, in addition, limited its rush-hour service on the West Valley Freeway Flyer to trips in the peak direction (e.g., inbound in the morning, outbound in the evening). But in late 1962 LAMTA reversed its policy and established "reverse commuter" service in conjunction with the extensions of Route #35.

Political Strategy

The importance of political strategy in the transit scene today was discussed in Chapters 3 and 4. It was stressed that a transit company, in meeting government promotion, regulation, and pressure, could influence public policy directly through legislative access and persuasion, and/or indirectly by obtaining voter support for transit's policies and projects.

It has been shown that expressway bus service involves relatively little capital investment or numbers of riders. Thus, in contrast to rapid transit operations, the problems of government policy and political strategy were not significant in the case studies. But these questions were not entirely absent. For example, it may be assumed that the decisions of both Los Angeles and Chicago to put service quickly on the expressways were designed both to attract traffic and to obtain government promotion of rail rapid transit.

In Philadelphia, however, the regulatory and other governmental pressures were important, and as such warrant examination. In 1963 the Philadelphia Transportation Company occupied a unique position in the domestic transit industry. It was the largest privately owned mass transit company in the world, but it operated the city-owned subway system through an intricate system of leases and rentals.[17] In addition to the traditional regulation of rates and service by the State Public Utilities Commission, and periodical negotiations with the city over franchise extensions or financing capital improvements, the company was also subject to the regulation of a Service Standards Committee, formed by the city and the company to arbitrate questions of PTC service within the community.[18]

[17] For a description of PTC, see U.S. Congress, Joint Committee on Washington Metropolitan Problems, *Rapid Transit Systems in Six Metropolitan Areas,* prepared by Gunther M. Gottfeld, 86th Cong., 1st. Sess., 1959, pp. 18–24.

[18] In 1957 PTC and the City of Philadelphia agreed on a renewal of the 1907 franchise. PTC accepted a schedule of extended rental payments for the subways, agreed to defer dividends until 1959, and joined in the establishment of a Service Standards Committee to arbitrate service complaints. The city withdrew a longstanding suit on rental payments.

This blending of public and private enterprise had advantages and disadvantages for both the city and the company. The city benefited from PTC's operating efficiency (relative to other companies operating rapid transit) and a low fare structure, whereas the company had been able to finance capital improvements with the city's low interest rate credit. In addition, the city had made tax-supported improvements in the subway system which had attracted riders and cut expenses for PTC.

On the other hand, the decade 1953–1963 witnessed clashes between the city and the company over rates of fare, extent of service, dividend policy, and labor agreements. For example, the 1959 annual report of PTC charged:

> City representatives know that labor rates have been climbing steadily in recent years and that adjustments are unavoidable if there is to be fair treatment of transit workers and efficient uninterrupted transit service for the public. Once higher cost contracts are signed, however, city lawyers go all-out to resist company moves toward off-setting fare adjustments. This resistance even included the repudiation late in 1958 of a written pledge that a fare-rise application would not be opposed by the city if PTC labor costs went up, as they did at that time. . . . In persistently delaying regulatory processes, the city must bear responsibility for the harm inflicted on one of its most essential public service agencies. Your management has learned a hard lesson: that it is folly to commit to pay envelopes money not yet in the fare box.

During this same period there were strong pressures for acquisition of PTC. In 1956 a city-financed study recommended that a regional transportation organization assume management and control of the transit system.[19] The report also urged that the Philadelphia urban area preserve its investment in rail commuter facilities. As a result, the city and subsequently three surrounding counties began a program of subsidized railroad commuter service.[20]

[19] Philadelphia, Urban Traffic & Transportation Board, *Plan and Program 1955* (Philadelphia: By the Board, 1956).

[20] For a complete review of the commuter service program and the agencies engaged in planning transportation for the Philadelphia area (in-

In July 1962 PTC's franchise was extended, and the newly elected mayor stated that he did not favor acquisition of the company. Following an extended transit strike in 1963, the pressures for acquisition were revived. In early 1964 the Governor of Pennsylvania signed legislation authorizing the creation of a Southeastern Pennsylvania Transportation Authority with the power to purchase, condemn, or lease transportation properties in Philadelphia and four surrounding counties.

The Ardmore express bus proposal pitted the transit company, supported by the Service Standards Committee, against the Pennsylvania Railroad and a representative of the city, who expressed his desire to be an intervenor in order to "ascertain the merits of the application for ourselves . . . [and] to guide the Service Standards Committee . . . in the future."[21]

The basic issue centered on the fact that the bus route paralleled in part the Pennsylvania's suburban railroad service to Ardmore. Inasmuch as the city had been subsidizing railroad commuter service on other lines, the railroad contended that the PTC bus route was contrary to the public interest, because it would divert rail riders rather than automobile drivers. After several days of hearings and over 400 pages of testimony the State Public Utilities Commission ruled in favor of PTC.[22] The railroad appealed to the courts, but the Commission ruling was upheld.

In the author's opinion, the strengths of the regulatory process lay in its role as an independent adjudicator of a highly emotional issue. But it is unfortunate that the parties could not have agreed beforehand on the relative place of the city, PTC, and the

---

cluding the disbanded Urban Traffic and Transportation Board, the Passenger Service Improvement Corporation, and the Penn-Jersey Transportation Study) see IRT, *Newsletter,* III (March 30, 1962).

21 *Pennsylvania Railroad Company* v. *Pennsylvania Public Utility Commission.* Record, Superior Court of Pennsylvania, October Term, 1962, No. 153, p. 55a.

22 *Ibid.,* p. 448a. The PUC was not impressed by the railroad's "time diversion curve" exhibits, which attempted to show that the bus would divert primarily rail, not automobile, riders and concluded that the joint bus service would eliminate inconvenience and waste, "all to the benefit and convenience of the public."

Pennsylvania Railroad in providing transportation to Ardmore. For the price paid for the privilege of the regulatory process was high. Not only was time, effort, and money expended for legal fees and research, but the start of the new bus route was delayed over six months pending the outcome.

It should be noted that the marketing strategy (complete, comfortable, direct central business district service) was an important element in securing the support of the downtown business community and potential riders who testified at the hearings, and in turn a favorable regulatory decision. Thus, a political strategy (in this case using the traditional regulatory process to avoid conflicts with the city over the question bus vs. rail) would seem to have greater effectiveness when reinforced by marketing decisions which produce grass roots support.

Formal Organization

In Chapter 2 a brief review of the formal organization of a transit company ventured the hypothesis that a transit company is production rather than marketing oriented, and therefore is organized by function rather than project or product. The expressway bus operations confirmed this observation.

In Los Angeles the key marketing decisions were initially made by the superintendent of transportation, a representative of the schedule department, an outside consultant, and the director of public relations. Chicago's Devon-Northwest Express was inaugurated following reports from the schedule department and traffic engineer. A "team" approach was used in Cleveland to plan the Bay Village extension,[23] whereas Philadelphia's Ardmore Express was developed in the planning department.[24]

---

[23] Cleveland's general manager believed strongly in committees as a means of determining and implementing policies. The Bay Village service was evaluated by the operating committee, which included representatives of schedules, transportation, personnel, the research director, and maintenance. This committee was chaired by the manager of operations (see Figure 2.2).

[24] The planning department performed the bulk of the research work prior to service extensions. It made cost and revenue studies, prepared special exhibits for regulatory proceedings, and monitored the results of approved new services. In 1962 the scheduling function was taken from the transportation department and placed under the director of planning.

Once the service was found to have attracted enough riders to "break even," the schedule departments, in most cases, took over the bulk of the marketing task, by monitoring patronage and adjusting schedules. Occasionally special studies were made by others within the organization (e.g., Los Angeles' postcard survey by the chief engineer's planning group or Chicago's Devon-Northwest extension study by the traffic engineer's staff).

But in no instance was one official given continuing formal responsibility for either the product (such as director of commuter operations) or the project (for example, director of express bus services). Because of the small scale of operation, however, one individual in each of the companies tended to keep "informal watch" over the bus line, in the person of either the superintendent of schedules, the director of planning, or a staff engineer.

Summary

In the expressway bus cases cited, the problems of formal organization and political skills do not appear to be as important or significant as marketing strategy. In general, the author felt that the marketing strategy decisions in most of the cases were quite appropriate for a service designed to attract suburban-CBD riders. These decisions included:

(1) A seats-for-all policy on long express routes.

(2) The use of nonstop express service to segregate short- and long-haul traffic, as well as to increase speed.

(3) The routing of express bus routes direct to the CBD.

(4) The use of zone and premium fares so as to offset the ceilings on revenues per trip caused by both seats-for-all and nonstop express trips.

(5) The strong initial promotional campaigns, and continued use of timetables, particularly when mailed seasonably to households.

On the other hand, the weaknesses seemed to be the failure to learn more about the riders and nonriders through market research, the absence of air conditioning to improve standards of comfort, and the tendency to view the potential patronage as those living within walking distance of the route. In turn, none of the lines attempted to develop or promote a park-ride operation in order to create the density of originating traffic needed for high volume profitable service.

The expressway bus operations studied showed the financial and operating problems of this form of service. On the one hand, the ratio of 50 seats to one driver requires high fares to sustain seats-for-all or nonstop express policies. On the other hand, expressway congestion and the need to operate in extended local pick-up zones lowers the average speed of operation to a point where it is not significantly attractive to the automobile driver.

It is difficult to reach any firm conclusions as to the ultimate ability of the bus alone to handle the mass transportation needs in our largest cities. As noted in this chapter, the battle between the bus and rapid transit advocates rages over the issues of relative cost, service, and attractiveness to the public. In this context, it is significant to find that each of eight transit executives responding to the author's questionnaire agreed that buses (even air conditioned) operating on freeways would be insufficient to reverse adverse traffic trends. Five of seven respondents felt, however, that rapid transit could reverse the declines in patronage. (Question 9)

We can now turn to an evaluation of management's attempts to market recent investments in rail rapid transit.

CHAPTER 6

Rail Rapid Transit

Introduction

This chapter will present and analyze four case studies of investments in rail rapid transit totaling over $100 million. The case studies were purposely chosen to report the most significant improvements in the rapid transit systems of Chicago, Boston, Cleveland, and Philadelphia at the time of the author's visit. It must be recognized at the outset that these cases have obvious dissimilarities. Chicago extended a rapid transit line using high-level loading equipment, but Boston's extension used low-level loading Presidents' Conference Committee (PCC) streetcars. Cleveland introduced a complete rapid transit system, but Philadelphia replaced only the equipment on an existing heavily traveled rapid transit line. Yet each investment is linked by similarities in the strengths and weaknesses in management's marketing and political strategies, and their ability to assign formal authority and responsibility for rapid transit marketing programs. As in the previous chapter, a brief synopsis of each case will precede the comparative tabulations of patronage and profitability and the analysis under topical headings.

Chicago Transit Authority: The Congress Service

In June 1958 the Chicago Transit Authority began operation of its Congress Service, "the first significant project providing rail rapid transit in the grade-separated right of way of a multilane expressway,"[1] thus fulfilling an engineering goal of integrating rail rapid transit and an expressway in one travel corridor. The 9.1 mile route connected with the Congress-Dearborn-Milwaukee subway just west of the Loop, and replaced the demolished Garfield Park elevated (Map). Congress trains were through-routed via the subway to Logan Square.

The rapid transit line featured modernistic stations (connected to the intersecting streets by ramps rather than steps), cars with transverse seats, and station loading areas designed to facilitate rapid transit-surface bus transfers. Although CTA management had been highly successful in obtaining city, state, and federal aid in financing the $33.2 million line as a part of the Congress Expressway project, they were unable to complete the "package" by including a major parking facility at the outer terminal or an express track in the sufficiently wide right of way.

Within a few months the rail line was widely heralded as carrying more riders at "30% of its capacity" than the adjoining highway at 100% during the peak rush hour, notwithstanding the fact that the highway cost four times as much as the rapid transit facility. This statistic should be clarified immediately. At Racine Station (1200W), the point where the traffic counts were taken, the Congress Service shared the same track with the Douglas Park line. Congress traffic alone was approximately 50% of the combined 10,300 person peak-hour Congress-Douglas traffic; thus the Racine location of the count favored the rapid transit.[2]

Aided in part by diverted riders returning from the paralleling Lake Street line,[3] Congress traffic grew both in the aggregate and

[1] City of Chicago, *Chicago's West Side Subway* (Chicago: By the City, 1958).

[2] Under the initial plan of service, Congress and Douglas headways were each 6 minutes during the peak hours, thus producing a combined headway of 3 minutes between Logan Square and Racine Station. It is clear that one-third capacity refers to "theoretical," not actual, operating capacity. Six-car trains at 3-minute intervals (120 per car) had a capacity of 14,400 persons. Longer trains could not be operated without lengthening the platforms of Logan Square, although capacity could be increased to 21,600 persons per hour by reducing headways to 2 minutes.

[3] Between September 1953 and June 1958 Garfield Park elevated trains operated over a slow ground level route because of construction of the Congress expressway. Many riders switched to the paralleling Lake St. line.

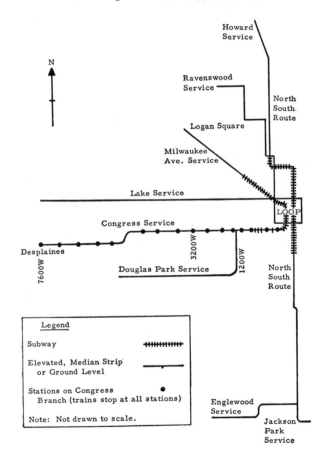

**Chicago Transit Authority:
Rapid Transit System**

relative to the remainder of the rapid transit system. But despite its national "image" of modernity and progress, certain statistics seem to indicate that the Congress line was more successful in attracting riders adjacent to the route than the suburbanites from the fastest growing sections of Chicago.

In a CTA survey taken in 1960 it was found that only 11.5% of the Congress riders had formerly used their automobiles for the trip in question, and that 50% of the inbound riders were able to walk to the stations rather than use buses or automobiles. In contrast to the Congress-Douglas peak-load statistics at Racine Station (1200W), over 60% of the peak-hour riders moving along the Congress Expressway corridor (Congress branch only) past Kedzie station (3200W) in 1961 were in automobiles. At Desplaines (7600W), the western terminal, the automobile's share of the market was even higher.[4]

Perhaps more striking is the statistic that while the combined Congress-Douglas trains were carrying approximately 70,000 persons into and out of the CBD between the hours of 7:00 a.m. and 7:00 p.m. in 1961, the Congress Expressway handled over 111,000 persons during the same period.[5] Of course many of these automobile patrons had origins or destinations that the CTA could not serve, yet it seems reasonable to conclude that substantial numbers of persons preferred the crowded highway to the new rapid transit line.

Metropolitan Transit Authority: The Highland Branch

Many transportation experts have suggested that much of the urban mass transit problem in our largest cities could be solved if

[4] A CTA count in 1957 showed 7,950 persons moving in the peak direction in automobiles during the peak hour at Central Park Avenue (3600W). In early 1963 CTA Chairman Gunlock testified at the Senate hearings on urban mass transit aid that Congress expressway automobile traffic during the peak hour carried 8,825 persons. CTA's Congress line traffic at Kedzie (3200W) based on a March 1960 survey, adjusted by the author to 1961, was 5,000 persons and patronage at Desplaines (7600W) during the same period was approximately 1,100 persons.

[5] Chicago Transit Authority, *Analysis of City of Chicago Cordon Counts* (Chicago: CTA, 1961).

rapid transit lines were built between the central business districts and circumferential expressways on the outskirts of the central cities. Investment costs would be reduced by utilizing existing railroad rights of way for the rapid transit lines. Parking facilities would be provided along the routes to attract CBD-oriented commuters living in the suburbs.

On July 4, 1959, Boston's Metropolitan Transit Authority[6] did just this by beginning operations over a rapid transit route between the CBD and Route 128, a belt expressway 12 miles from the center of Boston. The line utilized 9.4 miles of the abandoned right of way of the Boston & Albany Railroad's Newton Highlands Branch and cost about $1 million per mile excluding equipment. Almost 2,300 parking spaces were provided along the route, primarily at Woodland and Riverside (Map).[7]

The original timetable showed rush-hour and base-period headways of 10 minutes from Riverside, augmented by 10-minute rush-hour turnback service between Reservoir Station and the CBD. Inasmuch as this schedule provided a maximum of 24 two-car trains during each two-hour peak period, it would appear that the MTA anticipated a maximum of 3,600 riders each peak period, 50% of whom would originate east of Reservoir.[8] Assuming that at least 50% of the total daily traffic would originate during the four peak hours, it seems reasonable to estimate that the MTA anticipated an absolute maximum of 14,400 daily riders. From the first day when 20,000 tried to get on the cars it was clear that the magnitude and character of the traffic had been

---

[6] There are an extraordinary number of studies and reports describing and analyzing the MTA. For a recent bibliography, see Commonwealth of Massachusetts, Mass Transportation Commission, *The Boston Regional Survey, A Bibliography of Planning Studies,* prepared by the Planning Services Group (Boston: By the Commission, 1962). *The Boston Region,* pp. 117–154, contains an extensive description and analysis of the MTA. As discussed in Chapter 4, the MTA was absorbed by the Massachusetts Bay Transportation Authority in late 1964. This case study pertains to the MTA as it operated in 1962.

[7] Much of the descriptive data are taken from IRT, *Newsletter,* I (November 4, 1960).

[8] Assume 75 passengers per car, 48 cars each peak two hours.

Metropolitan Transit Authority:
Highland Branch Rapid Transit Service

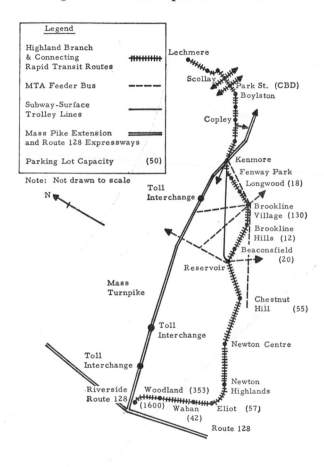

Legend

Highland Branch
& Connecting
Rapid Transit Routes

MTA Feeder Bus

Subway-Surface
Trolley Lines

Mass Pike Extension
and Route 128 Expressways

Parking Lot Capacity (50)

Note: Not drawn to scale

N

Lechmere

Scollay

Park St. (CBD)
Boylston

Copley

Kenmore
Fenway Park
Longwood (18)

Toll
Interchange

Brookline
Village (130)

Brookline
Hills (12)

Beaconsfield
(20)

Reservoir

Mass
Turnpike

Chestnut
Hill (55)

Toll
Interchange

Newton Centre

Toll
Interchange

Newton
Highlands

Riverside
Route 128

Woodland (353)

(1600)

Waban
(42)

Eliot (57)

Route 128

inaccurately estimated. Over 60% of the daily and 65% of the rush-hour riders boarded west of Reservoir.[9] As a result the MTA had to add signals (to permit reduced headways), a power substation, increased storage space at Riverside, and substantial rolling stock to the line. Service was increased, and the turnback trips to Reservoir were discontinued.

In 1960 the Greater Boston Economic Study Committee made a survey of the 6,000 daily riders boarding the Highland Branch beyond Reservoir.[10] The study found that 36% of the riders had two or more automobiles, 45% had family incomes greater than $10,000, and 48% had listed their occupational classification as professional, technical, scientific, management, or official.[11] Thus, at the outset the line appeared to be highly successful in attracting a class of patrons not normally associated with rapid transit. At the same time it was reported that 37% of the sample had formerly used an automobile for the trip being taken and that 40% of all riders boarding between Riverside and Reservoir lived in towns outside the MTA district.[12]

On the other hand, the survey found that many of the occasional riders complained of slow or uncomfortable service. The Mayor of the suburb primarily served by the outer half of the

[9] Commonwealth of Massachusetts, *Report of the Joint Special Legislative Committee on Transportation*, House of Representatives No. 3400, January 1962, p. 68. [Hereafter cited as *Mass. House 3400*.]

[10] Greater Boston Economic Study Committee, *A Study of Commuters on the Highland Branch* (Boston: By the Committee, 1960).

[11] By contrast, a 5,500 telephone interview survey made in late 1963 in the 22 United States metropolitan market areas of one million or more in population found that: (a) only 14% of the adult mass transit riders came from households whose annual income exceeded $10,000; (b) only 22.9% were professional, technical, managers, etc.; and (c) only 19.4% owned two or more automobiles. See *The Transit Millions*, prepared by Sindlinger & Company, Inc., for the Transit Advertising Association, Inc. (New York: By the Association, 1964). It should be noted that the telephone introduced a bias toward persons with relatively higher incomes; thus even the reported profile may not be accurate.

[12] The MTA District referred to the City of Boston and 13 other cities and towns surrounding the core, which received MTA service and shared the cost of annual deficits. In the vicinity of the Highland Branch (Map), the District was roughly defined by Route 128, the circumferential highway.

line echoed these complaints, calling the PCC streetcars "Toonerville Trolleys."[13]

An illustrated pamphlet handed out at the start of the service contained this message from the Trustees of the MTA ". . . The Highland Branch brings to Newton and Brookline [both within the MTA district] and the adjoining areas the fastest and most economical public transportation available today. It is our hope that the parking facilities . . . will serve the commuters' needs and be an added incentive for those people in the fringe areas of the MTA district to use our facilities. . . ." By October 1962, however, the Mass Transportation Commission found that only 670 automobiles used Highland Branch parking lots daily. At that time only 205 cars were parked at the Riverside lot.[14] An MTA passenger count taken during the same month showed 2,341 riders boarding at the outer two stations (Riverside and Woodland). This amount was 35% of those boarding west of Reservoir.

Assuming that riders living outside the MTA district would most likely board at Riverside and Woodland, and that at least a portion of those actually boarding lived within the MTA district, it seems reasonable to conclude that the percentage of Highland Branch patrons residing outside the MTA district declined from 1960 to 1962. In addition, the inability to utilize the parking lot at Riverside fully seems to indicate that the MTA had not been completely successful in attracting long-haul riders from the suburbs.

As a part of the aforementioned Mass Transportation Commission-HHFA demonstration grant, the parking fee of 35 cents at Riverside and Woodland was reduced to 10 cents in October 1962. The average daily number of cars parked by October 1963 rose to 514 at Riverside and 360 at Woodland, leaving 30 vacan-

[13] Donald L. Gibbs, "Problems of the Cities," *Proceedings of the 1961–1962 Series of Citizens Seminars on the Fiscal, Economic and Political Problems of Boston and the Metropolitan Community* (Chestnut Hill: Boston College, 1962), p. 141.

[14] Commonwealth of Massachusetts, Mass Transportation Commission, *Demonstration Project Progress Report No. 5—Tentative Conclusions* (Boston: By the Commission, 1963) p. 49.

cies at Woodland and 1,086 vacancies at Riverside. Thus, by the end of 1963 the promotional parking fees had raised the over-all occupancy of the six lots along the Highland Branch from 30% to 53%.

Following a fare increase toward the end of 1961, which raised the abnormally low fare structure to more realistic levels, traffic on the line fell from its 1960 peak of 30,000 to slightly more than 24,000 riders per day by October 1962.

Competition for this traffic promises to grow more severe within the next two years. Work is nearing completion on a $215 million 12-mile extension of the Massachusetts Turnpike toll expressway between Route 128 and the heart of downtown Boston (see Map). The expressway promises a 15-minute travel time between the CBD and Route 128 compared to the Highland Branch's 35 to 45 minutes. Although the combination of toll fees, automobile out-of-pocket operating costs, and downtown parking charges for one driver will be slightly more than four times the MTA fare, the difference diminishes to about 10 cents per passenger per day if as many as three persons join the automobile driver.[15]

It appears to the author that unless significant improvements are made in the speed and comfort of the rapid transit service, large numbers of the Highland Branch's riders will switch to the toll road, seriously depleting MTA revenues and leaving a substantial investment in fixed plant and equipment unutilized.

Cleveland Transit System: The Cleveland Rapid

At the time of the author's visit, Cleveland's $40 million rapid transit line (known locally as the Rapid) had several distinctions. It was the nation's newest rapid transit system, in contrast to extensions of existing routes in New York City, Chicago, Boston,

[15] Assume parking cost of $1.50 per day, auto operating cost of 5 cents per mile (out-of-pocket expenses), toll costs of $1.00 per day, round-trip automobile distance of 24 miles, an MTA parking fee of 10 cents and MTA round-trip fare of 80 cents. Before May 1963 the MTA parking fee at Riverside was 35 cents, but was reduced to the 10 cent level after the HHFA experiment.

and Philadelphia, and was the only one of the rapid transit systems financed solely from internal funds or revenue bonds.

In comparison with the three other cases studied by the author, the Rapid featured the greatest number of on-line parking spaces (5,962) and a unique form of express operation, begun at the insistence of the general manager. Finally, because of the round about nature of the line east of Union Terminal (Map, page 92), and its single downtown stop, CTS continued to operate express buses in competition with the Rapid, with its excellent timetables showing the advantage of using the Rapid for some trips and express buses for others.

Following its inauguration in 1955, traffic rose 79% by 1960, aided by a 1.8-mile extension (complete with 3,800 free parking spaces) and the institution of express service. By the summer of 1962, in part because of a fare increase, patronage had fallen about 6% to an average of 56,400 per day.

A 1961 cordon count by the City of Cleveland showed that between the hours of 7:00 a.m. and 7:00 p.m. the Rapid's share of the entering and leaving traffic had risen to only 9.6%. During this same period approximately 329,600 persons entered and left by automobile, with 92,932 of these traveling during the hours of 7:00–9:00 a.m. and 4:00–6:00 p.m. in the peak direction.

Traffic growth on the Rapid was hampered by two unresolved problems—a downtown subway, and the question of future extensions. Although the voters of Cuyahoga County approved a 1953 bond issue for a downtown subway (only 21% of the major downtown business area was conveniently served by the one station), the county commissioners killed the project. In addition to this setback, a major policy split developed between the five-man transit board (appointed by the mayor) and the general manager as to the method of financing rapid transit extensions.

Philadelphia Transportation Company: Introduction of New Rapid Transit Equipment

During the last six months of 1960 the Philadelphia Transportation Company replaced its entire fleet of antiquated rapid transit cars serving its 12.5-mile Market-Frankford line (Map, page 94) with 270 attractive stainless steel, high performance units, at a cost of $24.4 million. Their purchase culminated almost three years of intensive negotiations with the City of Philadelphia, which owned about half of the Market-Frankford route. Although the cars were financed with city credit, PTC was committed to repaying the full cost of the equipment.

Table 6.1 indicates that the Market line was the only segment of the PTC high level loading rapid transit routes to show an increase in patronage between 1959 (the last full year prior to the new equipment) and 1962. Had historical trends continued, the 1959 total of 68.6 million riders (including transfer passengers) would have dropped to 65.9 million by 1962, but the annual figure actually climbed to 71.1 million. Although evidence does exist to show that increased residential construction in northeast Philadelphia played a part in the favorable trend, it seems reasonable to conclude that the attractive, fast (the running time was cut 16%) cars played the major role in both maintaining existing riders as well as increasing patronage.

Unfortunately, in contrast to the new equipment, the stations along the Market-Frankford route, in the author's opinion, were among the dreariest and most unattractive in the United States. Many, including some of the busiest, were unequipped with escalators in 1962.

A 1955 cordon count indicated that 437,000 persons left the CBD during a 24-hour period by automobile or taxi, with 42,521 traveling during the peak rush hour (5:00–6:00 p.m.). The preliminary findings of the Penn-Jersey study reported that in 1960 41% of the daily trips made into the CBD were in private automobiles versus 40.6% in 1955.

In 1962 Philadelphia's commuter railroad subsidy program (6.2 million riders) cost the city almost $2 million. Although the city had spent considerable sums modernizing its wholly owned Broad Street subway (although not the equipment), it had not made similar expenditures on the Market-Frankford route. Until such time as the city and PTC agree on a program for financing station improvements, the Market-Frankford line will continue to be a blending of the old and the new in its most exaggerated sense.

Table 6.1

Philadelphia Transportation Company:
Percentage Change in Rapid Transit Patronage,
Selected Months, 1959–1962
(1959 = 100)

Month	Market-Frankford	Broad Ridge	Difference in Percentage Change*
January			
1959	105	104	+1
1960	99	98	+1
1961[1]	108	110	−2
1962[2]	107	103	+4
April			
1959[3]	104	106	−2
1960	102	100	+2
1961	104	101	+3
1962	105	97	+8
July			
1959	92	91	+1
1960	87	83	+4
1961	90	84	+6
1962	94	85	+9
October			
1959	104	105	−1
1960[4]	103	102	+1
1961	111	105	+6
1962	111	104	+7
December			
1959	115	108	+7
1960	126	120	+6
1961	112	99	+13
1962	110	96	+14
Annual[5]			
1959	100	100	0
1960	101	100	+1
1961	106	102	+4
1962	103.5	96	+7.5

* + indicates Market-Frankford percentage change more favorable.
— indicates Broad-Ridge percentage change more favorable.
[1] 22 cents unchanged; 5/$1 to 5/$1.05. Also one day strike, January 15.
[2] 22 cents to 23 cents; 5/$1.05 unchanged.
[3] Fare increase in March 1959—20 cents base unchanged; 5/90 to 10/$1.90.
[4] 20 cents to 22 cents; 10/$1.90 to 5/$1.
[5] Passengers include base fares and transfers.
SOURCE: Company records.

Patronage and Profitability of Rapid Transit Routes

Patronage

Although the rapid transit cases in this study represented investments far in excess of the expressway bus operations cited in the previous chapter, the scale of operations of the rapid transit lines was much greater. Table 6.2 shows the 1961 or 1962 peak-hour loads of the four rapid transit routes. The three high level loading rapid transit lines (Cleveland, Philadelphia, and Chicago) handled between 5,000 and 18,000 persons during the peak hour, the equivalent of three to nine expressway lanes, whereas on three of the four bus routes approximately 350 riders per peak hour were carried. Even the PCC streetcar-equipped Highland Branch of the MTA carried almost twice the peak-hour loads of Chicago's Devon-Northwest Express, the heaviest of the expressway bus routes studied.

The data indicate that after initial increases in traffic, only Chicago's Congress line was able to maintain its growth (albeit at a reduced rate) into 1962. The declines in Cleveland and Boston were in great part caused by fare increases in 1961. Philadelphia's relatively poor performance was deceptive. Its low rate of growth reflected both a much higher base volume and the fact that there was no extension into a new territory, only the replacement of equipment. As noted, its significance was the over-all 3.5% increase in traffic between 1959 and 1962 versus a 4% decline on the other major Philadelphia high level loading rapid transit line.

Profitability

Determining the profitability of a rapid transit route is much more difficult than doing so for express buses, for, as seen in the Chicago case in Chapter 5, a major question is the allocation of revenues received from a combination surface-rapid transit rider to the bus or rapid transit operation. In addition, it is sometimes impossible to allocate systemwide rapid transit costs to particular routes.[16]

[16] For an excellent discussion of other difficulties in costing rapid transit operations, see Lang and Soberman, pp. 125 ff.

Table 6.2

Patronage: Rapid Transit Systems, Study Cities

Nature of Statistic	Chicago (CTA)	Boston (MTA)	Cleveland (CTS)	Philadelphia (PTC)
Typical patronage per week day	58,700[1]	24,322[2]	56,400[3]	252,086[4]
Initial % change in traffic	1958–60 +39%	1959–60 +15.0%	1955–60 +79%	1959–61 +6%
More recent % change in traffic	1960–6/62 +19%	1960–62 −19%	1960–62 −5.5%	1961–62 −2%
Recent patronage in peak direction during peak hour on typical week day	5,188[5] (1961)	1,527[6] (1962)	7,200 (1962)	18,000 (1962)

[1] Estimated by the author based on total passengers boarding trains at Congress stations during the first six months of 1962. These totals were doubled to determine total daily trips, but double counted insofar as persons boarded at any of the Congress stations for a westbound, not an eastbound, trip. For example, a 24-hour peak-load count taken in 1960 and adjusted by a factor to March 1962 showed 49,300 daily riders at the peak-load point.

[2] Based on the average of a two-day on-and-off check of Highland Branch stations in October 1962.

[3] Based on the average number of persons boarding at all stations during the month of October 1962.

[4] Estimated by the author based on total boarding passengers for the year 1962.

[5] American Transit Association reported 10,376 peak-hour riders at Racine Station in 1961. Congress traffic was 50% of this combined Congress-Douglas traffic.

[6] Actual peak loads were much higher because (1) this was an average figure for a two-hour count, and traffic peaked within the two hours, and (2) the checkpoint was along the Highland Branch proper. Highland Branch trains carried substantially higher loads within the Boylston Street subway between the CBD and the beginning of the Highland Branch at Fenway Park station (See Map). In addition, congestion within the Boylston Street subway (Highland Branch shared tracks with four other PCC routes) resulted in "bunching" with some Highland Branch trains jammed to capacity and others only half filled.

Table 6.3 indicates that a reasonable allocation of revenues in Cleveland and Philadelphia was sufficient to cover all operating expenses and contribute to depreciation and fixed charges. The data from Chicago are much harder to interpret, because Congress revenues were lumped with those of Douglas and Milwaukee, and system average costs were used. It seems likely that the Congress Service was covering its total operating expenses, although not contributing substantially to depreciation or fixed charges. In contrast, Boston's Highland Branch, which operated under the unfavorable motorman per car labor cost-seat ratio of PCC streetcars, showed both an operating and a capital deficit in 1960. A major fare increase on the line in 1961 raised revenues perhaps as much as 25%, and may have reduced the operating deficit. The MTA has released no information on this subject since 1960.

We can now turn to consider the decisions of transit management and public policy which helped produce the existing patterns of demand and profitability.

Rapid Transit Marketing Strategy

Pricing Policy

As was the case with the express buses studied, each of the four rapid transit routes had a different fare structure. Both Philadelphia and Chicago charged the systemwide flat fare, although CTA instituted a 5-cent transfer charge to connecting surface buses in 1961. Cleveland collected a 5-cent premium over its base fare for a rapid transit trip, the same policy as on its express buses. Boston's MTA was the only one of the four to use a zone fare (varying from 10 cents to 40 cents).

The rapid transit fares were not significantly low. The rider in 1962 paid between 2.63 cents (CTA) and 4.22 cents (CTS) per mile on trips from the closest outer terminal to the central business district, the same range as found in the express bus case studies. The CTS fare (as well as Philadelphia's 3.83 cents per mile charge) included the privilege of transferring to most connecting feeder buses.

Table 6.3

Comparative Financial Results: Rapid Transit Systems, Study Cities

City	Comment
Chicago	A controller's study for the five-month period January-May 1960 concluded that revenues of the complete West-Northwest service (Congress, Douglas, Milwaukee) covered all operating expenses (including the payment to the city for the fixed facilities of the Congress route) and contributed to the systemwide depreciation and fixed charges. However, if one-sixth of the revenues were credited to surface vehicles, the contribution to depreciation and fixed charges disappeared. Revenues used in the study were the maximum possible, i.e., 24.28 cents per passenger times the total passengers, even though a significant number of rapid transit riders paid their fares on surface buses before transferring to the rapid transit.
Boston	In 1960 revenues of the Highland Branch failed to cover operating expenses (including overhead) by $338,000 The inclusion of fixed charges raised the loss to $804,000. Revenues were increased by the 1961 fare adjustment.
Cleveland	In 1961 the excess of revenues over total operating expenses (excluding certain minor taxes, depreciation, and fixed charges, but including allocated overhead) varied between $493,000 and $3,163,000, depending on the allocation of revenues to surface buses.
Philadelphia	In 1961 total revenues (based on the published average revenue per passenger on the Broad Street line of 10.4 cents) covered total operating expenses (excluding depreciation and fixed charges) by about $76,000. The revenue figure used implied a substantial allocation of revenues to surface vehicles, inasmuch as the system fare was 23 cents (8 cents for students). In addition, the author estimated that in 1961 the incremental revenues from new and retained riders almost covered the annual capital costs of the new equipment.

SOURCE: Interviews, annual reports, and A. Scheffer Lang and Richard Soberman, *Urban Rail Transit* (Cambridge: MIT-Harvard Joint Center for Urban Studies, 1964), p. 77.

Although the price policies, except in Boston, generally produced revenues sufficient to cover operating expenses, some of the fare structures had perhaps unintended consequences on the complete marketing package. For example, Cleveland's Rapid had very poor CBD distribution because of the one station at the Union Terminal. Yet CTS continued to maintain a historical 3-cent transfer charge between the Rapid and local "Loop" buses in the downtown area. This resulted in East Side rapid transit riders paying 3 cents more per trip than East Side express bus patrons to those sections of the CBD beyond walking distance from the Union Terminal. The charge also slowed the Loop bus service because of the difficulty in making change and handling pennies. Perhaps in its effort to collect a 3-cent transfer fare on the Loop buses, CTS was making the rapid transit service less attractive and losing 30-cent fares. In short, if feeder buses must be used to provide CBD circulation (thus overcoming a deficiency in the original rapid transit designed route), it might be unwise to hamper this bus service with a small transfer charge.

In July 1961 Chicago inaugurated a systemwide 5-cent transfer charge rather than raise the 25-cent flat fare. As a result, the rider who had taken notice of CTA's promotional campaigns to make a combination surface-rapid transit trip found himself paying more for this kind of trip as opposed to riding a surface route (either local or express) through to the CBD.

Finally the MTA's fare increase of 1961 produced a problem of fare collection on the Highland Branch. The zone fare required all outbound riders to leave by the front door of the car. Subsequently, the average speed from terminal to terminal during rush hours dropped from 17.12 to 16.2 mph, slower than many express bus operations in other cities.

Market Research Policy

Inasmuch as rapid transit is characterized by heavy expenditures of money, large volumes of passengers, and the need to seek government financial aid for new projects, it is not surprising that the author found more rapid transit market research studies than was the case with the express buses. These studies included peak-load counts, percentage analyses of ridership by hours of the day at the peak-load point, on and off counts at each station, analyses of CBD cordon counts, attempts to forecast patronage by counting households in the service area, postcard surveys of riders, and even license plate checks to determine the origins of patrons using rapid transit parking lots.

Market research was at its best when it led to improvements in service and patronage. For example, on and off counts in Cleveland along the West Side stations led to the establishment of a unique form of express service. Their analysis of parking lot patronage and license plate checks resulted in the expenditure of several hundred thousand dollars to provide parking space along the West Side line. A CTS planning team used market research effectively in developing proposals for extensions of the Rapid.

In Chicago an extensive analysis of station-by-station patronage was made by the staff engineer to support a plan for skip-stop express service on the Congress route. Postcard surveys were also used to determine the potential demand for expanded parking facilities at the end of the Congress line. Unfortunately, neither an express plan nor expanding parking facilities resulted from the studies.

Forecasting naturally is subject to uncertainty. As noted, Boston's MTA erred in predicting the traffic on the Highland Branch. Not only did the MTA have to invest funds in new signals and equipment, but it found itself subjected to the criticism of the State Auditor for failure to do a better job of forecasting.[17]

Aside from errors in forecasting, the author found two major weaknesses in the marketing research programs. At times he got the feeling that except for the routine peak-load counts (which were vital in determining headways and lengths of trains), many of the statistics were developed simply for the sake of continuing historical tabulations, rather than for use in improving the service or attracting riders. But more important, too many of the

17 *Mass. H. 3400*, pp. 67 ff. The auditor was a frequent critic of MTA policies. Under the authority of the MTA's enabling legislation, he was empowered to audit the MTA's financial statements annually.

rapid transit statistics were analyses of actual riders; not enough work was being done on who was not riding rapid transit, and why.

One improvement lies in better coordination with the transportation studies now under way in many of the cities, yet the author found that in most cases existing procedures and coordination have failed to produce significant exchanges of information. Several transit officials in the cities visited expressed a lack of confidence in the "3% samples" used by city planners. Yet these "3% sample" origin-destination studies can enable transit management, for the first time, to learn rapid transit's "share of the market" along major traffic corridors. With these data, realistic patronage targets can be set, new routes and services planned, or existing service adjusted.

Promotion Policy

Rapid transit promotional policy can be compared to a semi-successful moon shot. At the outset, there is a great deal of fire, smoke, and noise as the missile is launched. For a short period of time, information is relayed back to the ground, but then the "batteries go dead" and nothing more is heard.

In each of the rapid transit examples described above, a tremendous amount of excellent publicity preceded and accompanied the opening day of the service, utilizing the press, radio, TV, pamphlets, and advertising. At times the publicity was almost too good, for the promises of "Jet Age" travel did not always materialize. Yet once the line was in operation, the promotional effort dropped off to occasional news releases ("100,000 riders passed through the turnstiles today setting a new record") or writing a descriptive article for national publications.

One reason for the drop-off might be that management assumed that the potential riders knew of the line's existence (and its price, headways, running time, etc.), and therefore concluded that extra promotion (such as timetables, advertisements) would be a waste of money. The author disagrees, and believes that in particular timetables can be quite valuable (as demonstrated on the express bus routes) in giving information on connecting feeder buses and rapid transit train departure times.

Chicago published an excellent booklet in early 1962 showing maps, headways, and running times of each route on the rapid transit system. Copies could be obtained by writing to the public relations department.

When the Highland Branch opened, the MTA handed out timetables at the stations along the line. These showed headways only at the outer terminals, plus running times to intermediate stations, and required some involved calculations to estimate the time of arrival of a train at a given station en route. But, unlike Chicago's booklet, they could easily be kept in a wallet or tacked on a wall for reference. In common with the Chicago booklets, they included no detailed information on feeder bus connections. The MTA timetables were discontinued in 1962 because of an economy drive, but were restored using a more readable format in March 1964.

Cleveland's rapid transit promotion strategy represented a significant contrast. Timetables were published for every feeder bus route, with not only the time of arrival of each trip at major intersections en route, but also the connecting rapid transit train and time of arrival at the CBD terminal. These timetables were regularly mailed to a list of 100,000 homes.

Cleveland has shown that the costs of mailing and printing timetables were low in comparison with the system gross revenues. One method of achieving the personal contact with the homeowner, yet reducing these mailing costs even further, might be to coordinate with other firms that do periodic large mailings, such as department stores or utility companies.

Perhaps another reason that promotion dies after the "kick off" is that the public relations director feels that he has nothing to sell. Unfortunately in many cases this seems to be true. This leads to the consideration of product planning as a component of rapid transit marketing strategy.

Product Planning Policy

Loading Standards: One of the major findings of the preceding chapter was that several companies, recognizing the importance of comfort in diverting automobile riders, had successfully instituted a "seats-for-all" policy on some of their expressway bus routes. It is interesting to compare this progressive marketing strategy with the rapid transit cases. In each of the case studies, the rapid transit rider was promised "modern commodious cars" or "Jet Age travel" as the new line was opened or new equipment was introduced. What standards of comfort did he find?

Table 6.4 reports the ratio of peak rush-hour loads (after all, the rush-hour rider is rapid transit's best customer) to available seats on the four routes studied by the author. The peak-load point, where the counts were taken, varied from route to route. On CTA's Congress line the counts were taken at Racine Station only 5 to 7 minutes west of the Loop, whereas the MTA Highland Branch counts were taken at Brookline Village, 15 to 20 minutes west of Park Street (CBD) during the rush hour.

It is clear that each line carried a substantial number of standees at the peak-load point, particularly when it is remembered that each of the statistics was understated, because there was a peak 15 minutes within the peak hour. It is reasonable to estimate that during the rush hour each route carried standees for at least 40% to 60% of the trip. Thus, the loading standards on these "new modern" routes were not much different from those on other rapid transit lines in the same cities.

The contrast between these rapid transit rush-hour load factors and the seats-for-all policy on the expressway bus routes is obvious, and a natural question arises: Why should a rider be happy, crowded and standing in a rapid transit car, when it is recognized that he is unhappy, crowded and standing in a bus?

Transit officials give several explanations for the common load factors of 150% to 200% during the rush hour on rapid transit lines:

(1) The trip usually does not take much time; therefore the rider does not mind standing.

(2) The rider would rather stand in a rapid transit car than fight automobile traffic and pay high parking fees.

(3) It would cost too much to provide seats-for-all in rapid transit.

The first point seems valid for those extremely heavy routes, relatively close to the CBD, whose riders generally are unable to

Table 6.4

Comparative Standards of Comfort: Rapid Transit Systems, Rush Hour at Peak-Load Point, Study Cities

Nature of Statistic	*Chicago (CTA)*	*Boston (MTA)*	*Cleveland (CTS)*	*Philadelphia (PTC)*
Seats per car	50	42	53	56
Standees per car	70	58	47	84
Potential Seated, capacity per peak hour	4,500[1]	2,520[2]	9,540[3]	11,424[4]
Potential Seated and Standing, capacity per peak hour	10,800	6,000	18,000	28,560
Actual Seated, capacity per peak hour (1962 schedules)	3,300[5]	1,890[6]	4,664[7]	8,736[8]
Actual Seated and Standing, capacity per peak hour	7,920	4,500	8,800	21,840
Reported peak-hour loads (Table 6.2)	5,188	1,527	7,200	18,000
Per cent reported peak-hour loads to actual seated capacity	157%	80.8%[9]	154%	206%

[1] 6-car trains, 4-minute headways. The Congress stations could accommodate 12-car trains, but because the trains were through-routed to Logan Square, their length was kept to 6 cars to fit into the cramped Logan terminal.

[2] 3-car trains, 3-minute headways. Length of trains limited by congestion in Boylston Street PCC streetcar subway.

[3] 6-car trains, 2-minute headways. Platforms designed so that they can easily be lengthened to accommodate longer trains.

[4] 6-car trains, 1.75-minute headways. Trains can be coupled to 10 cars, but platform lengths prohibit this.

[5] 6-car trains, 5.5-minute headways.

[6] 3-car trains, 4-minute headways.

[7] Based on 30-minute check—two 6-car and eight 4-car trains.

[8] 6-car trains, 2.3-minute headway during peak hour.

[9] Peak loads on many trips much higher. See Table 6.2, note 6.

make the same trip by automobile. Common examples are many of New York City's routes. But this argument does not appear to apply to the long-distance suburban commuter who can enjoy a seat on an express bus or in his automobile rather than stand in crowded rapid transit cars.

Therefore, the transit industry, stressing traffic congestion and the capacity of transit to handle large loads (mostly standing), uses the second argument toward the potential automobile driver which implies: "We may be bad, but the automobile is worse." Although the commuter may put up with this "lesser of two evils" approach for a while, it is logical to assume that he will not have strong sympathies for the transit company and will press for more highways or decentralization of economic activity to avoid having to use transit in the long run.

There is no denying that a seats-for-all policy at existing fare levels could be costly. Such a policy would require either increasing the seating capacity of cars, operating longer trains, or increasing train frequencies.

It might well be feasible to experiment with the first method by installing 3–2 transverse seating on long suburban rapid transit routes (which are most subject to highway competition). The disadvantage would be increased loading and unloading time, but this need not be serious if the great majority of the riders traveled to one or two central business district stations. Budd's "Pioneer III" railroad commuter coach has been designed for 3–2 seating within an over-all car width of 10 feet, and one recent study has estimated that at least 79 seats could be provided in existing modern rapid transit cars.[18]

Unfortunately in many cases long trains are prohibited by short platforms in stations. New York City has recently undertaken a major program of platform lengthening to enable operation of 10-car trains. On the other hand, where platform lengths are sufficient, increasing the length of trains would minimize incremental operating costs per passenger, for except in the case of Boston's PCC's, labor costs would not increase.

[18] "This Car May Well Be It," *Trains*, XVII (November 1956), pp. 42–47 for data on Pioneer III. See also Meyer et. al., Tables I and B 3, which indicate that on the basis of 4.79 square feet per person, the Philadelphia and Cleveland rapid transit cars could seat 79 persons.

Increasing train frequency would cause the greatest increase in operating expenses. On the other hand, the recent HHFA railroad commuter demonstration project in Boston suggested that commuters strongly favor increased service (and seats) and will tolerate increases in fares to support expanded levels of service.[19]

It is significant to note that the San Francisco Bay Area Rapid Transit District has promised to move 30,000 seats per hour past a given point during the rush hour, thereby insuring a seat for the vast majority of the riders. It seems reasonable to assume that this was a major selling point in convincing the community to support the project through district taxes.

Existing rapid transit systems may not be able to afford the costs of increased train service, modification of equipment, or lengthening of platforms. An alternative method of providing seats-for-all would be to operate certain rapid transit lines at higher standards of comfort but charge premium fares, exactly in the same manner as express buses. This possibility will be examined shortly under the heading "segregated long-distance express service."

Air Conditioning: The cases in this and the preceding chapter were developed by the author with the objective of reporting and analyzing new and progressive developments in mass transit. Yet none of the vehicles in any of the cases was air conditioned, although Philadelphia, Cleveland, and to a certain extent, Boston, operated sealed-window rapid transit cars with ventilating fans. This absence of air conditioning is perplexing, for air conditioning appears to be one of the easiest and least costly means of improving the "image" of mass transit.

Consider the typical transit trip during a day when the temperature rises into the low 90's. Every city visited during the trip has several, and often a dozen or more, such days each year. The bus or rapid transit car is hot and crowded. The drivers and conductors are uncomfortable and irritable. The atmosphere is repressive. These unpleasant days are the ones remembered by the transit rider, not the far greater number of times transit takes him from his home to destination safely, reasonably

---

[19] *Massachusetts Demonstration Project Progress Report No. 5*, p. 13.

quickly, and cheaply. There is no need to elaborate on the contrast between an air-conditioned vehicle, even when crowded, to the normal transit vehicle ventilated by open windows or fans.

In view of this reluctance to include air conditioning in the transit "product," the author included two questions on the subject in his questionnaire. The first question (Question 10) asked the chief administrative officer the following:

> Following a fare increase, your company was able to improve its net income position last year. As you evaluate your capital budget, you find that you will have $200,000 to spend on capital improvements that you had *not* counted on. Which of the following would you tend to spend the money on? (Please rank in order)
> ( )   Air condition 44 buses of your fleet of 800.
> ( )   Make improvements in your maintenance facilities.
> ( )   Invest in securities, that is, set up a fund for contingencies.
> ( )   Purchase seven new buses.
> ( )   Increase the advertising budget by $200,000.
> ( )   Use the money to support experimental extensions of service.

Each of the executives indicated that his first choice would be to purchase seven new buses. The remaining choices, in order of importance were: (2) improve maintenance, (3) set up fund for contingencies, (4) experiment with extensions of service, (5) air condition, and (6) advertise. Three of the six respondents put air conditioning down as their most unfavorable choice, although one official indicated that he would rank air conditioning just behind new buses.

The answers are significant for they show that management is most likely to make capital improvements which will make the production task easier. New buses not only mean possibly more riders but, more important, reduce maintenance and operating costs. Likewise, the administrators wanted to improve maintenance facilities, or simply "save for a rainy day." Undoubtedly, the prospect of air conditioning was unpopular not only because of increased maintenance costs, but simply because it was felt that air conditioning was not needed in their city.

This crucial point of the need for air conditioning as a part of the marketing package was stressed in the next question (Question 11):

Your company operates in a city where the maximum temperature during June, July, and August usually exceeds 85 degrees. Although the city is not a "southern" city, it is generally agreed that "during the summer months, it is a pretty uncomfortable place to live." You operate a fleet of 1,000 buses, 200 of which are over 10 years old. Your average operating cost per bus mile is 70 cents. You presently have no air-conditioned buses. Your base service is covered by 400 buses and your peak service uses 950 buses. To air condition the buses would cost $4,500 per unit and increase maintenance and operating costs by 1.75 cents per bus mile. Which of the following would you *most* likely do: (Choose one) (Assume you have adequate borrowing capacity at 4% interest.)

( )   Air condition your total fleet of buses.

( )   Air condition the base fleet of 400 buses only.

( )   Use the funds for some other purpose.

Although the question was purposely phrased to make it appear that the city in question was hypothetical, in reality, each of the respondents was from a city which could fit the description in the question. Yet of the eight respondents, five said that they would air condition only the base fleet of 400, three reported that they would use the funds for other purposes, but *not one* chose to air condition the total fleet, even though the funds were available.

Thus the majority in effect said: "Even if I have the money, I will not invest in equipment which is going to be idle a good part of the day. I will be content to have over 50% of the rush-hour fleet not air conditioned, even though I recognize that the climate warrants air conditioning of the base fleet." This is like the owner of a motion picture theater installing an air-conditioning system sufficient to keep customers comfortable during the middle of the week, but insufficient to handle more than 50% of the load on Saturday night when the theater is filled.

In the author's opinion, the responses to the questions on air conditioning were completely consistent with the production orientation of top management in the industry. Faced with a myriad of operating problems and always operating under cost constraints, the transit executive leans to decisions which will enable his company to perform its day-to-day job in the most efficient manner possible. He will avoid investments in "frills" or marketing "gimmicks," particularly if they also mean increased maintenance or operating costs.

Recently there has been a marked change in the attitude of some transit executives toward air conditioning. During 1963 both the Chicago Transit Authority and the Port of New York Authority ordered air-conditioned rapid transit cars. San Francisco's rapid transit equipment, likewise, will be air conditioned. Pittsburgh's Allegheny County Port Authority ordered 150 air-conditioned buses in early 1964.

The Chicago purchase shows the extremely modest incremental cost of air conditioning new equipment. CTA ordered 180 rapid transit cars (semi-permanently coupled into 90 two-car sets) at an aggregate cost of $18,990,000. The incremental cost of the air conditioning was $5,000 for the two-car set or 2.4% of the cost of nonair-conditioned equipment.[20]

Bus air-conditioning costs are somewhat higher. In 1962 air conditioning added $4,600 to the cost of a $30,000 diesel bus. Operating and maintenance costs, however, were quite low. They fell within a range of 1 cent to 1.5 cents per mile for maintenance, and 0.75 cent to 1.0 cent per mile for increased fuel consumption. These figures were only a small fraction of the typical total bus operating costs of 60 cents to 75 cents per vehicle mile.[21]

Despite the orders in Chicago, Pittsburgh, and New York City, there is still evidence that the industry has not wholeheartedly swung over to air conditioning. During 1963 the New York City Transit Authority and Boston's Metropolitan Transit Authority received new nonair-conditioned rapid transit equipment. The New York City "World's Fair" cars were advertised in early 1964 as "the most modern new cars available today."[22] It would appear to the author that if transit continues to shun tangible marketing improvements such as air conditioning in the name

[20] Letter to the author dated January 17, 1964, from Mr. David Q. Gaul, Executive Secretary, Institute for Rapid Transit.

[21] Robert J. Wilson, "Analysis of Transit Coach Air Conditioning" (unpublished report, General Motors Institute, 1962), pp. 66–114, and letter to author from Mr. E. W. Hall, Advertising Manager, Motor Coach Division, GMC Truck & Coach Division, General Motors Corporation, dated May 23, 1962.

[22] *New York Times,* April 5, 1964, Sec. 11, p. 3.

of economy, the "image" of transit will remain one of cheap, uncomfortable service, primarily designed for low income groups or for those who cannot drive a car.

Escalators: A final point in connection with standards of comfort should be mentioned briefly. Subway and elevated stations are perhaps the only remaining locations in the urban community where large numbers of persons have to climb many steps. Fortunately, the installation of escalators by many transit companies is eliminating this problem. Yet it is obvious that the potentially large market of senior citizens, who generally cannot drive, is deterred from using rapid transit not only by overcrowding, but especially by the steps in the stations.

Speed: It is not an exaggeration to say that we live in an era that worships speed. How else can one explain the expenditure of hundreds of millions of dollars to develop a supersonic airliner, or to design automobiles capable of cruising at 90 mph? The very name "rapid transit" implies speed. Indeed, on an express train of the New York City subway system, speed is quite apparent as the train hurtles past local stations at 50 miles per hour. But what about rapid transit lines in cities other than New York?

Table 6.5 shows that the 1962 rush-hour rider traveled at an average terminal-to-terminal speed varying from 16.2 to 28.4 mph. Of course, this did not include the time spent transferring to slow feeder buses at the end of the trip or, alternatively, walking to an automobile in a parking lot. This does not seem like "Jet Age" travel. Indeed, except for Cleveland's Rapid, average speeds were less than 23 mph, only slightly better than the terminal-to-terminal express bus runs cited in the previous chapter.

There were three reasons for the low average speeds. Either (1) the stations were spaced too closely together, (2) no express track was provided, or (3) all trains operated as locals.

Table 6.6 shows that except in Cleveland the 1962 distance between stations was less than one mile. It should also be noted that the MTA and CTA extensions of existing subway lines ended short of the CBD. In the Dearborn (Chicago) and Boylston

Table 6.5

Comparative Standards of Speed:
Rapid Transit Systems, Rush Hour, Study Cities

Nature of Statistic	Chicago (CTA)	Boston (MTA)	Cleveland (CTS)	Philadelphia (PTC)
Distance from CBD to outer station	9.5 miles[1]	11.61[2]	7.8 ES 7.1 WS	6.5 NE 6.0 WS
Fastest time from CBD to outer station—rush hour	26 min.	43[3]	17 ES 15 WS	19 NE 18 WS
Average speed—CBD to outer station, mph	21.9 mph	16.2 mph	27.5 ES 28.4 WS	20.5 NE 20.0 WS
Express service	No	No	Yes[4]	Yes[5]

[1] Although the Congress route was only 9.1 miles long, the distance between the principal CBD stations and the start of the Congress line (via the Dearborn subway) added about 0.4 mile to the trip.

[2] Although the Highland Branch proper was only 9.4 miles long, it reached the CBD (in common with several other PCC routes) via the Boylston Street subway. The 11.61 miles was the total distance between Riverside and Park Street.

[3] In all cases except the MTA, the off-peak running time was about 2 minutes faster than the peak hour shown in the table. However, because of difficulties in fare collection and congestion during the peak hour in the Boylston Street trolley subway, the normal MTA running time (off-peak) of 35 minutes was increased to 43 minutes.

[4] The CBD was in the middle of the CTS route. WS stands for West Side and ES for East Side. The express service ran nonstop between the CBD and the outer West Side stations, bypassing three stations en route.

[5] The CBD was in the middle of the PTC route. WS stands for West Side (to 69th Street) and NE stands for Northeast (to Bridge Street). During rush hours, skip stop "A," "B" service eliminated 25% of the station stops for each train.

Street (Boston) subways stations were spaced even more closely than on the extensions. This short station spacing places severe restrictions on average operating speeds. One recent study found that the average terminal-to-terminal speed with high performance rapid transit cars (acceleration 3 mphps, top speed 70 mph) making intermediate stops of 30 seconds' duration would be 25 mph with stations spaced at two thirds of a mile. With one-mile

Table 6.6

Station Spacing: Rapid Transit Lines, Study Cities

	Chicago (CTA)	Boston (MTA)	Cleveland (CTS)	Philadelphia (PTC)
Length of route (miles)	9.1	9.4	14.9	12.5
Stations (1962)	15	13	14	28
Average distance between stations (miles)	.61	.70	1.06	.45

SOURCE: Company interviews.

station spacing, average speed would increase to 31 mph. If stations were spaced at two-mile intervals, average speed would be 43 mph.[23]

The only way that rapid transit lines not possessing multiple track can improve these low average speeds is to have certain trains skip stations and in effect lengthen station spacing. When CTA had been unable to finance an express track in the sufficiently wide right of way on the Congress route, one of its engineers proposed an express train plan. Under his proposal every other train would operate as an express bypassing three lightly patronized stations en route. Two to three minutes would be cut from the anticipated 23-minute running time. Inasmuch as the Congress branch trains were operating on a 6-minute headway during the rush hour, the lightly traveled stations would be subject to a 12-minute headway. There were several objections raised. The transportation department objected to the complicated operations resulting from four classes of trains on the West Side line[24] and noted that such a plan might create a strain on

[23] Lang and Soberman, p. 43.

[24] The four classes would be: Congress Local, Congress Express, Douglas Local, and Douglas Express. Headways on the Milwaukee segment would be 3 minutes; thus the headway for the Congress Local west of the Douglas junction would be 12 minutes. The complexity of four-class service was reminiscent of the Garfield Park elevated operation. At that time CTA operated express trains during both rush and base hours from Westchester, Desplaines, and Laramie. Not all express trains stopped at the same stations, and even during different times of the day a "Westchester Express" might serve different stations.

the three-track Logan terminal. They said that transportation experts across the nation would be watching the new line and pleaded for as simple an operation as possible. The general manager agreed with the objections but stressed that Congress headways should not exceed 10 minutes. In addition, there was a general spirit of "let's wait and see how the traffic develops." Therefore, the express-local plan was rejected and the Congress line opened with local service. As a result, the travel time between the Loop and the Desplaines terminal actually exceeded the express service which had once operated over the former Garfield Park elevated.[25]

In 1962 the staff engineer again reintroduced his express plan for the Congress and Douglas branches, because a new station at Kostner Avenue was about to be opened on the Congress leg. He noted that the average boarding per station on the three lightly traveled stations on each branch was approximately 30% of the totals boarding at the other stations, and that the average number of boarding passengers per car was less than 1.2. He commented that "such light station traffic reduces rapid transit to the character of bus operation at these points." His 1962 proposal advocated that every third train operate as a local, with the express trains saving at least 3 minutes per trip. With respect to the time saving, he said that many riders on CTA's other skip-stop routes felt that they were saving up to 15 minutes per trip, where in reality they saved only 4 or 5. Again the express plan was rejected.

In contrast, Cleveland's general manager (who was called by one official the "best schedule man in the United States") insisted on express train service for the West Side line when service was extended from West 117th to West Park station. Despite the skepticism of some in the transportation department, a schedule was prepared whereby express trains operated every 6 minutes during the rush hours, bypassing three stations enroute to West Park. A local was sandwiched between each express on a 1 to 2 minute slower running time. Checks showed higher loadings per

---

[25] The Chicago, Aurora & Elgin interurban electric railway used Garfield Park tracks to reach the Loop. No stops were made between Desplaines and the CBD. Eastbound running time was 24–27 minutes, and westbound running time was 20–22 minutes.

car on express trains than the locals, as well as an increase in the share of the Rapid's total traffic by the stations served by the express trains. Significantly, the 28.4 mph average speed of the West Side expresses was the highest rush-hour performance of the four lines studied.

PTC also used skip-stop during the rush hours to overcome its extremely close station spacing. Twenty-five percent of the Market-Frankford stations were bypassed by each skip-stop train, raising the average speed to 20.5 mph. But in the case of Boston's MTA, no express service was operated on the Highland Branch's single track.

The importance of speed cannot be overemphasized. For example, one transit research study released in late 1962 concluded that if transit travel times equaled those of the automobile, 32% of the high income, 50% of the moderate, and 88% of the low income groups would make their central business district-oriented trips by transit.[26]

Segregation of Short-Haul and Long-Haul Traffic: Table 6.7 presents data showing the percentage of the total weekday traffic boarding at the outer two stations of each of the four lines studied. When it is considered that most of those who board at the stations return the same day to the same station, it can be concluded that a significant proportion of the total weekday traffic on each of the four lines was "outer terminal oriented."

Table 6.7

**Importance of Outer Two Stations
on Rapid Transit Routes, Study Cities**

Company	Date of Check	% of Total Weekday Traffic Boarding at the Outer Two Stations of the Route
CTA	Nov. 1960	11.0 (Desplaines and Harlem)
MTA	Oct. 1962	9.6 (Riverside and Woodland)
CTS(WS)	May 1962	14.6 (West Park and Triskett)
CTS(ES)	May 1962	17.6 (Windermere and Superior)
PTC(NE)	Year 1962	13.6 (Bridge and Margaret)
PTC(WS)	Year 1962	9.3 (69th and Milbourne)

[26] *1962 Capital Region Transportation Plan*, p. 58.

The importance of this outer terminal patronage suggests that where operating conditions permit, efforts should be made to run nonstop express rapid transit trains from the CBD to the outer stations.[27] These express trains would provide faster and more comfortable service for the substantial numbers of riders using the outer stations, as well as attract new suburban riders because of the absence of annoying stops en route. This was one of the major attractions of the Cleveland West Side express which served only the outer three stations of the six-station line.

Segregation of long- and short-haul rapid transit performs another major function. Rapid transit best handles CBD-oriented traffic. In turn, one study has noted that the CBD daytime population will consist of high-income managerial personnel, medium-income secretarial and white collar workers, and low-paid unskilled labor from minority groups. The study goes on to say:

> Accordingly, a mass transportation system of the future, if it is to be efficient, should cater to two very opposite poles in the spectrum of social and economic classes. On the one hand, there would be the high-income executive, technical types and their secretaries; on the other, there would be the unskilled labor used in service industries and mainly recruited from minority groups. Past experience suggests that it may be very difficult to get these rather diverse groups to travel in the same vehicles.[28]

Clearly "such diverse groups" can be handled by transit by putting them in separate vehicles, such as local and express buses. But it is also true that in certain cities segregation of long-

----

[27] This assumes that the majority of the outer terminal riders are destined for the central business district. Unfortunately, origin-destination data by station origin were not available in all cases. A 1958 survey of West Side riders in Cleveland (before the line was extended from W. 117th to West Park) found that 61.2% of the riders from the outer two stations had CBD destinations. In 1960 the Greater Boston Economic Study Committee reported that 77% of the inbound riders from the outer half of the Highland Branch had CBD destinations. On the other hand, a 1959 CTA survey of the total Congress branch found only 43% of the riders with CBD destinations. Yet it still seems reasonable to hypothesize, particularly in the light of railroad commuter experience, that as distance from the CBD increases, rail transit riders will tend to be more CBD oriented.

[28] Meyer et. al., p. 38.

and short-haul rapid transit traffic can also produce a segregation of persons of different social classes and income, which might well prove attractive to suburban riders.

Finally, nonstop express trains to the outer stations would be best suited for a premium fare seats-for-all service. In most cases it is impossible to collect a premium fare on rapid transit trains because of the difficulty of identifying and segregating premium fare passengers. But on nonstop express trains the premium can be collected en route or paid when entering and leaving the outer stations. In the latter case, either separate platforms or gates could easily separate the local from the express traffic at the outer terminal. Thus the suburban "status package" would be complete: premium speed, premium comfort, and premium price.

Convenience—Parking Lots: In Chapters 2 and 3 the author pointed out that mass transit (particularly rapid transit) thrives when land use patterns create high densities of travel between two points. Usually the central business district is an important destination for work or shopping trips, and it is obvious that transit's future rests heavily on the continued attractiveness of the downtown area.

On the other hand, the dispersal of residential locations into the suburbs has destroyed many of transit's most lucrative routes because of the lowering of the density of residential population. One method of restoring density of mass transit travel is to extend rapid transit routes toward the suburbs and use feeder buses to bring riders to the rapid transit stations. Unfortunately, feeder bus operation is extremely costly and often not profitable.

The alternative is to have the transit rider perform his own feeder service and use parking lots at rapid transit stations to create artificial densities of originating residential traffic.

As noted, Cleveland and Boston have invested heavily in parking facilities along rapid transit lines. Although Boston's Highland Branch lots were not used to capacity, Cleveland's lots along the West Side line at Triskett and West Park stations (capacity 3,800 cars) were filled daily. A 1959 survey of these two Cleveland stations found that almost 30% of those using the free lots had formerly driven their automobiles the length of the trip. It is not surprising that because of the parking lots and express service, patronage at West Park and Triskett continued to grow into 1962 in the face of a slight decline in the aggregate Rapid traffic.

On the other hand, as of 1962 Chicago had been unable to provide more than 580 spaces the full length of its Congress route. The 500-car lot at the Desplaines terminal was filled at 6:45 each morning, and a member of the public relations staff commented: "How can we promote park-ride when we have no parking spaces?" In this respect, it is interesting to recall that a 1960 survey found only 11.5% of the inbound Congress riders had been diverted from automobiles.

Philadelphia had also recently improved its modest parking program. The Market-Frankford line in 1962 had 335 spaces at the 69th Street terminal and 525 spaces at the opposite Bridge terminal. The city hopes to increase both lots to 1,000 capacity.

One major question is the desirability of charging a parking fee. If the lot is well located and not too large, it can be filled each day even though a fee is charged. An excellent example was Philadelphia's 69th Street lot at the western terminal of the Market-Frankford rapid transit line.

But if a fee results in unused parking lot capacity, there are several good reasons for consideration of free parking. If a lot is not filled, the transit company may lose more from round-trip rides not taken than it gains from parking revenues. The 1963 Mass Transportation Commission demonstration project found that by reducing the parking fee from 35 cents to 10 cents at the large Riverside lot on the Highland Branch, monthly gross income increased from $7,100 to $14,600, even though the lot still was being used at less than one third of its capacity.

Large free parking lots such as in Cleveland may be a cheaper substitute for expensive feeder bus service. Also, the collection of parking lot fees may hamper entry and egress from the lot. Traffic has to funnel past one collector, and if volumes were as heavy as transit executives hope, the jams could be as serious as those on expressways. It would appear that park-ride plans cannot reach their traffic potential if the "park" element of the plan discourages the automobile driver.

A final point centers on the argument that free parking lots might be used by persons who have no intention of riding the transit lines. It would seem that in the suburban areas this problem would be minimal, since most suburban plants provide their own parking facilities. If garages are built, they will have controlled entrances. The facility could be designed to force the parker to exit via the rapid transit turnstile.

In short, the transit industry might well note the success of the suburban shopping centers with their free parking lots, from the point of view of both flow of traffic and the psychological attraction of "getting something for nothing."

A Proposal for Modern Rapid Transit

What should be the elements in a truly modern rapid transit system, one that would both capture the imagination of the community and divert substantial numbers of persons making trips in the urban areas by automobile?

For the moment, let us consider the impact of an investment in marketing CTA's Congress line. Contrary to normal engineering practice, a third track would be installed between Desplaines and the mouth of the subway near Halstead Street, even though the existing tracks are not at capacity. The logic behind the third track would be the same as that of a passing lane on a highway; not to increase capacity but to increase the speed of some of the vehicles traveling the route.

Nonstop express trains would operate between Desplaines and the Loop stations, both during the peak hours for commuters and occasionally during the base period for shoppers, at average speeds of 40 mph to 45 mph, cutting the running time to the Loop to 15 minutes or less. The cars should be air conditioned and suitably identified by signs, pennants, etc., with a name that catches the eye of the public (e.g., "Congress Jet").

The parking area would be modified to handle large numbers of "Kiss-Ride" parkers, dropping off and picking up their husbands. Particular attention would have to be paid to the problem of traffic flow into and out of the Kiss-Ride area. Feeder buses would be timed to connect with the express trains, and timetables would be mailed to homes in the service area showing both the feeder bus trip times at major intersections and the arrival time in the Loop via the express train.

The cost for power, signals, and track (estimated by the author based on a 1962 Cleveland feasibility study of a 7-mile double track line) would range from $3.5 to $4 million.[29]

In 1962 approximately 1,300 persons boarded the Congress line at Desplaines during the peak hour,[30] while 5,000 to 7,000 persons moved past the station in automobiles on the expressway. It thus seems reasonable to assume that the demand for the nonstop express service could reach a total of 3,000 persons during the peak hour. CTA could handle this potential demand in one of several ways, depending on policy decisions with respect to loading standards (all seated versus 50% standees), length of trains, and fares.

It would be pointless to develop detailed costs of such an investment without a full-scale feasibility study which would evaluate the service according to theoretical schedules and the service and price parameters mentioned above. However, preliminary rough calculations by the author seem to indicate that the incremental revenues from 3,000 round trips (at a premium fare of 50 cents one way) would more than cover operating expenses and the capital costs of air conditioning, track, and signals.[31]

In the author's opinion, this investment would enable CTA riders to enjoy truly modern rapid transit for the first time. The dramatically fast, air-conditioned equipment would blend the speed and comfort of railroad commuter service with the con-

[29] Cleveland Transit System, *Southwest Rapid Transit Extension to Brooklyn-Parma Area* (Cleveland: CTS, 1962), p. 6.

[30] A check in November 1960 showed 4,700 persons boarding at Desplaines and a survey in March 1960 indicated that about 23% of the total inbound riders at the peak-load point rode during the peak hour. The author has estimated the figure of 1,300 persons based on these factors adjusted to 1962 by applying a growth factor of 19%.

[31] It is assumed that CTA would buy new equipment anyway if demand increased. The incremental costs would be only the air conditioning, track, signals, and modification of the station at Desplaines. In the author's preliminary calculations, more intense utilization of the equipment by off-peak shoppers would increase the contribution to company overhead.

venient CBD distribution and low fare of rapid transit. CTA's public relations department could advertise without hesitation that the new express rapid transit service would provide comfortable, fast, cheap, and convenient urban transportation.

Perhaps the suburban automobile driver would "buy this new product." Certainly, CTA's "image" to the general public would improve, and there might be less hostility to CTA's plans for public financial aid.[32]

Political Strategy

In the preceding chapter a brief look was taken at the relationship between the government and transit. In that instance it was found that marketing decisions helped the Philadelphia Transportation Company obtain approval of its new express bus service via the regulatory process. Rapid transit, however, in contrast to express bus operations, requires heavy capital expenditures, much of which may have to be supplied by some agency of the government. Thus, the ability of transit management to secure a complete rapid transit marketing package requires the formulation of a political strategy to obtain government promotion. This section of the chapter will illustrate the kinds of problems that require the transit manager to use political as well as administrative skills, and will emphasize the interrelationship between marketing and political strategy.

Initial Financing and Design of Rapid Transit Facilities

The case studies revealed both successes and failures in the crucial stage of getting the government to finance important

[32] In April 1964 CTA initiated nonstop rapid transit service between Skokie, Illinois, and the Howard Street terminal of the North-South rapid transit line utilizing an abandoned portion of the Chicago, North Shore & Milwaukee right of way. In one sense, this nonstop $6\frac{1}{2}$-minute service resembled the author's proposal inasmuch as the rapid transit trains achieved rates of speed in excess of 50 mph with an average speed of about 40 mph. Initial patronage of 4,650 riders (4,000 of which were new to CTA) exceeded expectations. The "Skokie Swift," however, offered no through service to the Chicago CBD. As of the fall of 1964 it remained to be seen if this Housing and Home Finance Agency demonstration experiment could cover its costs.

design features. Chicago's Congress Street line is perhaps the best example of a fusion of many political interests into an agreement on a financial plan. Table 6.8 shows the breakdown in the costs of constructing the facility.

Table 6.8

Costs of Construction: Chicago's Congress Street Expressway and Rapid Transit Line

(In millions)

Section	Expressway Including Rapid Transit	Rapid Transit
Within city[1]	$106	$23.8
West of city[2]	66	9.4
Total	$172	$33.2

[1] The $106 million cost was shared equally by the city, Cook County, and the State of Illinois (whose contribution was supplemented by federal matching highway funds). The city paid the $23.8 million cost of fixed transit facilities.

[2] The $66 million cost was financed jointly by Cook County and the State of Illinois with their contributions supplemented by federal matching highway funds. Of the $9.4 million cost of the rapid transit line, the state's share was $6.4 million and the county's $3 million.

Source: CTA

CTA assumed the cost of removing the Garfield Park elevated structure, spent $2.7 million acquiring fixed transportation equipment rented from the Chicago Aurora & Elgin Railroad plus land and terminal properties at Desplaines Avenue, and agreed to reimburse the city $11.7 million over a period of 31.67 years for the costs of tracks, signals, and interlocking equipment. The use of federal highway funds to help finance the extra highway costs in connection with the rapid transit (e.g., longer overpasses) set a precedent and signified a major change in federal highway financing policy.

A CTA promotional booklet listed no less than 15 cooperating groups representing the city, Cook County, the State of Illinois, and the U.S. Bureau of Public Roads taking part in the project.

CTA's ability to obtain federal as well as state and local financial aid was an outstanding example of working through the political process to finance rapid transit.

On the other hand, in each of the cases the transit company was unable to persuade the government to finance a complete modern rapid transit "package." For example, if a rapid transit line is to serve persons who cannot make the same trip by automobile, or who live relatively close to the proposed route (e.g., high density apartments), the design might well feature relatively closely spaced stations, located at major cross streets served by surface buses.

But if the line hopes to attract automobile-oriented suburban riders (and the publicity in each of the cities stressed this objective), it must include good CBD distribution, platform lengths sufficient for 8 to 10-car trains, and either (1) an express track or (2) stations spaced at least one mile apart (preferably both) to insure high speed service. Once the design features are determined, it is up to transit management to provide the quality of service discussed in the previous sections of this chapter.

It is easy to see, in view of the above criteria, that the design of the Congress route, perhaps forced on CTA by the city (which paid for the stations) as a replacement of the Garfield Park elevated, had neither the express track nor adequate station spacing, and thus could not provide the high speed service needed to attract the suburban rider with local trains alone. Failure to secure extensive parking facilities at Desplaines, again a question of public policy, further weakened its ability to divert automobile drivers.

On the other hand, Cleveland had adequate station spacing (which partially compensated for the lack of an express track) and parking lots. But its one downtown station made it more comparable to a suburban railroad because of the poor CBD distribution.

In 1953 CTS succeeded in having a proposal for a $35 million downtown subway loop put on the ballot. Under the financing plan the County of Cuyahoga would issue general obligation bonds and CTS would lease the subway. On the same ballot was a $4.5 million county office building. The voters approved the subway by a 2 to 1 majority, but voted down the office building. (Subsequently the office building was constructed from general funds not subject to voter approval.)[33]

Despite the affirmative vote, the county engineer called for an engineering feasibility study of the subway loop. In 1956 the engineering firm reported that the subway was feasible, but the county engineer convinced the county commissioners to delay the project, pending his own study. In 1957 he issued a report strongly criticizing the use of county funds to finance the subway. The general manager of CTS countered this report with his own study. In it he alleged that the county engineer had "misstated, misquoted, misinterpreted, and misjudged" persons and data.[34] However, the county commissioners, by a 2 to 1 vote, failed to issue the bonds.

In 1958 the City of Cleveland prepared a master plan for the renewal and conservation of the downtown area. Again the subway loop was included, although on a different alignment from that in the 1956 study. Hearings were heard on this proposal during 1959. The subway was strongly supported by the Cleveland Automobile Club, City Planning Commission, League of Women Voters, Euclid Avenue Association, and the press. However, there was some dissension within the downtown business community between those served by the existing rapid transit station at Union Terminal and those to be served along upper Euclid Avenue.

Again, by a 2 to 1 vote, the county commissioners killed the project, but in its place recommended a major study of the feasibility of the county taking over CTS. The theory was that if CTS wanted the county to finance capital projects, the county should operate a coordinated transit system.

The role of the county engineer in the blocking of the downtown subway should not be underestimated. He had been very active, though sometimes unsuccessful, in politics. He was once defeated (though backed by the Democratic Party) for mayor

33 IRT, *Newsletter,* II (November 15, 1961), p. 11.

34 Donald C. Hyde, *The Future of Metropolitan Cleveland Depends on the Downtown Subway* (Cleveland: CTS, 1957).

and ran third in the 1958 Democratic primary for governor.[35] He was also the man most identified with Cleveland's mushrooming expressway program.

In short, the resistance of the county engineer, the split in the downtown business community, and the lack of strong support from high elected officials (despite the voters' mandate) doomed the project.

The MTA's Highland Branch included parking lots and excellent station spacing in its outer half. But because of the MTA's chronic deficits and the consequent reluctance of the state legislature to approve costly MTA projects, the "bargain basement" rapid transit line used surplus, low loading, PCC streetcars and was built without an express track or fencing. The latter meant that the PCC's (top speed 42 mph) were further restricted to a maximum of 35 mph.

The Philadelphia Transportation Company also had difficulty with the community over the amount and method of financing capital equipment. The city initially suggested that 325 cars would be needed. PTC offered to purchase 190 cars at a cost of $17.7 million, but asked that the city finance the cars with PTC reimbursing the costs over a 30-year period. PTC proposed that the city purchase the remaining 135 cars for $12.6 million, and also lower the rental paid by the company for use of the Frankford Elevated to "reduce the large loss now being suffered from the operation of this service."[36] After three years of negotiations only 270 cars were ordered, with PTC repaying the full cost of the equipment through interest and rentals. The reduction in equipment made it difficult to improve loading standards through use of more trains.

Thus, failure to agree at the initial stages of design and finance of an investment in rapid transit on basic objectives, such as "Are we seriously trying to attract suburban-CBD automobile

[35] Dallas M. Young, *Twentieth-Century Experience in Urban Transit: A Study of the Cleveland System* (Cleveland: Western Reserve University, 1960), p. 24.

[36] Letter from Mr. Douglas M. Pratt, President of the Philadelphia Transportation Company, to Mayor Joseph S. Clark, Jr., of Philadelphia dated June 13, 1955.

drivers?" can mean defects in design which may never be completely offset by subsequent management marketing policies.

Financing Rapid Transit Extensions

In Chapter 5 it was found that Chicago's Devon-Northwest Express bus operation resulted from the inability of CTA to finance from internal sources an extension of the Logan Square rapid transit line out the Northwest Expressway plus the unwillingness of the state or local government to provide financial assistance. The following case raises the point that even when a transit system is able to generate investment funds, the question arises as to the best use of the funds.

In 1960 the Cleveland Transit Board directed the general manager to prepare a feasibility study of extending the West Side rapid transit line to the airport. Later that year the general manager reported that the airport extension would be able to cover its incremental operating costs, but not the $12 million capital costs. He recommended that the capital costs of the extension be supplied by the community.

The Board, however, passed a resolution conditionally committing the spending of funds from CTS' modernization reserve. This fund, established by the trust indenture, was maintained by an annual appropriation of 7% of the system's gross revenues. The general manager publicly stated that the replacement fund was barely adequate for normal replacement of facilities (new buses, maintenance facilities, etc.) and should be limited for the most part to such purposes. The annual appropriations to the replacement fund between 1959 and 1961 were $1.9 million, enough to purchase 60 new buses each year. But although the Board authorized purchase of 100 new vehicles in 1959, it bought only 30 buses during each of the years 1960, 1961, and 1962. As a result the balance in the replacement fund grew to $4.2 million as of December 31, 1961.

Shortly after his reappointment by the mayor, one of the Board members told the general manager during a weekly Board meeting that he ought to get in line on the airport extension or quit. The general manager replied: "If there comes a time when the Board is not interested in a good system and an efficient system, you can be sure I have no interest in being head. . . ."[37]

In July 1962 the general manager again requested 60 instead of 30 buses in order to convert a trackless trolley line to bus operation. It was estimated that the substitution would save $150,000 per year. The Board, by a 3 to 2 vote, turned down the proposal, and the general manager was quoted: "As long as the Board won't let management run this system efficiently, it must either raise fares or cut service, or both."[38] One of the Board members (of the majority) bitterly replied that neither would fares be raised nor service be cut. Subsequently, service was sharply reduced. In November 1962, however, the Board authorized the purchase of 60 buses for delivery in 1963. Also, in early 1964, the Board voted to move ahead on a partial extension of the West Side line toward the airport.[39]

Again, the failure of public officials to agree on basic questions of public policy with respect to transit promotion not only hampered the marketing of rapid transit, but also contributed to the kinds of executive board-career management friction described in Chapter 4.

The Transit "Image" and Political Support

During his trip the author made it a point to ask each newspaper reporter he interviewed what the people felt about the local transit company. The replies were not encouraging. The best that could be said was "apathetic, we don't have the best, but we don't have the worst." The comments then moved progressively downward to "outright cynicism and distrust." In view of these comments, it is not surprising that a politician gets far more "political mileage" out of attacking a transit company than of supporting it.

It is apparent from the financial statistics introduced in Chapter 2 that the transit industry will need substantial capital aid if it is going to provide modern transportation in our urban areas. Much of this capital aid will be used for rapid transit

[37] Cleveland *Plain-Dealer,* January 26, 1962.
[38] Cleveland *Press,* July 17, 1962.
[39] *Passenger Transport,* January 24, 1964, p. 1.

projects. Table 6.9 shows the present status of rapid transit projects in the study cities. Many of the proposals are stalled for lack of capital financing. The transit industry's ability to obtain such aid will depend upon the support it receives from the business and political communities, civic interest groups, and "the man in the street." As demonstrated in San Francisco, grass roots voter support (the feedback in flow chart—Figure 3.1) may prove decisive in determining the future of rapid transit and the transit industry. Of course, voter support in a referendum alone may not be sufficient, as was demonstrated forcefully in Cleveland. Elected officials must be willing to support transit, and this will most likely depend upon the general transit "image," itself a product of marketing strategy. In turn, the political process will more likely provide the capital aid needed for station modernization, express tracks, equipment, etc., to reinforce marketing strategy.

Formal Organization

The weaknesses in the formal organization of most (if not all) transit companies are clearly exposed in the analysis of the rapid transit cases. Consider, for example, the soap industry in contrast to transit. If an investment of $25 million were made in a new kind of soap, a project or product manager would be assigned continuing responsibility for coordinating the marketing and production of the new brand. It is likely that he would be supported by a staff organization parallel to functional officials in the company.

One of his major responsibilities would be to keep in close contact with the consumer, to handle promotion, forecast sales, and determine "the share of the market" of the new product as it moved from the production line to retail outlets. If sales did not reach anticipated targets, he alone would be responsible for explaining the reasons.

He would also maintain records of revenue and expenses, and if the accounting system allowed, produce periodic statements of return on investment for budget evaluation. Any problems, customer complaints, etc., concerning the new soap would be directed to him, which, in turn, might suggest major or minor

Table 6.9

Rapid Transit Projects: Study Cities, April 1964

City	Project	Cost (In millions)	Status
New York	.67-mile Queens-Manhattan tunnel	$ 30	A
	6.5-mile Manhattan express subway	197	B
	Chrystie-DeKalb-Sixth Ave. line	97	C
	Rehabilitation of Hudson & Manhattan by Port Authority	150	C
Los Angeles	64-mile rapid transit system	669	B
Chicago	10-mile northwest rapid transit extension	46	B
	Chicago Area Transportation Study recommendations	47.8	B
Philadelphia	3.0-mile northeast extension—Broad Street	65	A
	1.4-mile south extension—Broad Street line	20	A
	10.5-mile extension—Camden Line-Delaware River Port Authority	62	C
Detroit	No rapid transit proposals		
San Francisco	75-mile Bay Area Rapid Transit District	997.6	C
Boston	6-mile Malden extension	31.0	A
	Other extensions and rapid transit improvements	169.0	B
Pittsburgh	17-mile rapid transit system	94.0	B
St. Louis	$175 million express bus proposal only		
Washington	23-mile rapid transit and 15 mile commuter railroad plan	400.6	D
Cleveland	4-mile airport extension	13.0	C
	7-mile Brooklyn extension	17.3	B
	7-mile southeast extension	19.1	B
	5-mile northwest extension	11.2	B
Baltimore	Studies being undertaken		

A = Active planning stage or at least initial approval by government agency.

B = Proposed, but stalled for lack of financing.

C = Project now in progress.

D = Scaled down from original 83-mile rapid transit, 15-mile commuter railroad $793 million proposal. Stalled for lack of financing.

SOURCES: *Institute for Rapid Transit* and *Chicago Area Transportation Study.*

modifications in the nature of the product. In short, the new soap would be "his baby."

Compare the soap company with a transit company introducing a new rapid transit line. During the construction of the line an engineer is given formal or informal coordination responsibility. But once the route goes into operation, it is fused into the production-oriented functional routine.

There is a superintendent of rapid transit lines, but he is a production official whose responsibility is to see that the work force operates the trains in conformance with the schedule submitted by the schedule department. In view of the labor pressures described in Chapter 4, this official's time quite often is taken up with labor problems. He has no time to worry about questions of marketing strategy.

Which individuals are typically responsible for marketing the rapid transit investment? A list developed from the field trips included:

Pricing	Engineering, comptroller, finance
Promotion	Public relations
Market Research	Public relations, engineering, finance, planning department, schedules
Product Planning	
Speed	Schedules, engineering, supt. of transportation
Comfort	Schedules, engineering, supt. transportation
Parking lots	Engineering
Equipment	Engineering

What is missing in this list is a coordinating official either product-oriented (such as director of commuter operations) or responsible for the project (for example, Congress Service project director, or rapid transit lines' marketing director). In contrast to the express bus cases, cited in the last chapter, where the scale of operation was small enough so that one man (director of schedules or director of planning) could keep "informal watch" over all elements of the marketing mix, there was no one individual with continuing responsibility for marketing a rapid transit investment below the general manager or president.

This lack of formal responsibility for marketing coordination below the general manager is serious, for the general manager is often concerned with questions other than marketing. The author's questionnaire found (Question 1) that six of eight respondents spent more than 30% of their time on operating problems (including labor). Four of these, in turn, spent more than 50% of their time on operations. Yet four of these same eight men spent less than 10% of their time on marketing and public relations combined. Only one individual estimated that he devoted as much as 30% of his working hours to questions of marketing and public relations.[40]

In the absence of formal responsibility, coordination is achieved through staff meetings or committees. Yet the committee approach, though good for assigning temporary authority to "put out fires" and sharing ideas, still avoids the basic question: delegating continuing responsibility for a project. In addition, the committee or staff meetings tend to be dominated by the production-oriented transportation department ("Don't make our job any more difficult than it already is"). The only member with a marketing orientation (other than perhaps the general manager) is usually the director of public relations, and judging by the size of his budget appropriation his opinions often are not decisive.

Much of the day-to-day responsibility for the "marketing program" is entrusted to the schedule department, which seasonally reviews running times, makes peak-load checks, and adjusts headways. In the author's opinion, the schedule department is not the appropriate group to be deciding these questions of marketing strategy. It is a production-oriented group which takes the peak-load counts and produces an operating plan which meets this demand, yet balances the pressures of the comptroller and transportation department for lower costs and the union for longer running times.

The department rarely worries about the nature of the riders at the peak-load point (e.g., their origins and destinations) or

---

[40] Although the questionnaire was answered by executives of systems operating buses alone, as well as rapid transit executives, the data confirm the general problem.

why more persons are not riding. Although annual forecasts of rapid transit traffic are made, these are for budgetary purposes, rather than marketing. The forecasts lead to calculations of car-mile expenses, not "share of the market."

A few companies have recognized the pressures under which the schedule department works and have removed it from the control of the transportation department. An excellent example is Philadelphia's planning department, which handles questions of "market research" along with new routes, fares, changes in schedules, regulatory proceedings, etc. The director of planning now has formal authority over the schedule department and reports directly to the president. Yet even within this group no single individual has continuing responsibility for "marketing" the Market-Frankford cars, or, for that matter, coordinating the marketing effort of the rapid transit system. A major problem is the size of the staff. There are too many "fires to put out" and not enough people to do it.

If the transit industry could market rapid transit in the same excellent manner that it operates and maintains the trains, its "image" to the community would surely improve. But this will not take place without formal responsibility and authority being assigned for marketing the service in the same manner that responsibility is delegated for operating and maintaining the equipment.

Summary

There seems little doubt that the great majority of transit executives believe the industry's future in large cities depends upon the building of new rapid transit systems together with the modernization of existing rapid transit routes. Of the twelve sample cities only St. Louis, Detroit, and perhaps Baltimore are planning to rely wholly on buses for mass transportation. In many of the remaining cities, however, future rapid transit construction will require continuing substantial public support. Even the $375 million approved federal aid program will not be sufficient to finance the routes some experts believe are necessary to sustain intense economic activity in the core cities.

With this background in mind, it is important to recognize the weaknesses, as well as the strengths, in the rapid transit marketing and political strategies and to emphasize the importance of formal organization.

Management's rapid transit marketing strategies, as seen in the case studies, can be summarized as a series of dramatic contrasts. On the positive side were engineering achievements such as CTA's functional stations and integration of rail rapid transit into the median strip of an expressway and the MTA's successful conversion of the scenic Highland Branch to rapid transit.

These design features were augmented by important marketing decisions including the extensive parking lots in Cleveland and Boston, Cleveland's timetables and integrated feeder bus operations, the reasonably comfortable (though nonair-conditioned) equipment in Philadelphia and Cleveland, and the express service in Philadelphia and Cleveland. Yet the author believes that there were important weaknesses which seriously hurt the "image" of both the transit company and rapid transit. These included:

(1) Crowded rush-hour services, no different from other rapid transit lines. No seats-for-all policy.

(2) Slow rush-hour service, because of a lack of an express track, or failure to introduce express trains.

(3) No attempt to make the ride more comfortable by installing air conditioning. It is significant to note that Chicago's newest rapid transit cars to be delivered in 1964 will be air conditioned. Also, the Port of New York Authority and the San Francisco Bay Area Rapid Transit District promise air-conditioned equipment. On the other hand, Boston and New York City continued to take delivery of nonair-conditioned rapid transit cars during 1963 and 1964.

(4) A reluctance to eliminate historical surcharges (such as parking fees, transfer fares to "loop buses") even though the surcharge might deprive the company of the basic round-trip fare, as well as slow service, because of collection problems.

(5) A tendency for "market research" to stress descriptive statistics of persons riding the line, or measures of the capacity, rather than investigate why people were not riding rapid transit.

(6) Failure to invest in a continual personal promotional campaign designed to attract riders, as well as inform the community on questions of public transit policy.

Using the Congress line as an example, the author has suggested a way of improving immediately the rapid transit "image." This question of changing rapid transit marketing strategy will be discussed further in the concluding chapter.

Although the cases show the use of adept political skills during part of the initial design and finance process (especially in Chicago and Boston), it is also clear that management has not been able to gain the political support necessary to finance a complete "package" designed to attract both central city and suburban residents. Critical design features which have not been approved include station spacing, platform lengths, express tracks, parking lots, and escalators.

The rapid transit cases also illustrate the interrelationship between marketing strategy and political success. Merely demonstrating that rapid transit has the capacity to handle large numbers of riders in crowded, uncomfortable, slow trains will not win votes for the transit company, and thus will not win votes for the politician who supports rapid transit. It is no wonder, then, that the transit industry has experienced great difficulty in securing political support and the critically needed financial aid.

Perhaps the crux of the marketing and political problems lies in the fact that formal responsibility for these tasks is not delegated to individuals in the same way that authority and responsibility are assigned for the performance of "production-oriented" functions. The author will suggest changes in the formal organization to improve the "selling" of mass transit in the final chapter of this study.

CHAPTER 7

Conclusions and Recommendations

Introduction

This final chapter has three objectives. The first is to restate the author's assertion of the importance of marketing strategy by reviewing the analysis of the patronage and financial characteristics of the industry, the external pressures confronting it, and the spectrum of internal strategies being implemented by transit management.

The second is to draw together some conclusions from the literature, questionnaire, and field case studies and answer the questions posed at the beginning of the study. These were: (1) How successful have recent different marketing strategies been in terms of patronage and profitability? (2) What are the strengths and weaknesses of transit management's marketing strategies? (3) What is the interrelationship between marketing and political strategy? and (4) How does formal organization affect the success of marketing strategy?

The concluding section of the chapter will contain recommendations to public administrators, urban planners, and executives of the mass transit industry. As noted in the preface, the author freely admits a bias toward the transit industry. He was extremely grateful for the cooperation he received from transit officials during his trips, and he feels that these men are, in general, doing a good, conscientious job of planning and administering transit service despite a variety of pressures. In addition, the author favors a strong mass transit component of a balanced transportation network in our largest cities. The above sentiments, however, do not mean that the author agrees with all of management's policies in the cases studied. Thus, he hopes that any of the following conclusions or recommendations which imply faults in the existing practices will be read in a spirit of constructive criticism. In addition, the author recognizes that some of his suggestions may be more valuable as topics for further discussion and research; however, he believes that most of his recommendations could and should be implemented in the immediate future.

The Mass Transit Industry:
Patronage and Financial Trends

The mass transit industry is dominated by a small number of companies. In 1961 the twelve companies serving the twelve largest cities in the United States represented only 1% of the total number of companies in the industry, yet accounted for 52% of the revenue passengers. Because of the importance of scale in the industry, the statistical analysis in this study was arbitrarily confined to this sample of companies.

The New York City Transit Authority, however, stood out among these large firms. In 1961 it handled 81% of the total industry rapid transit riders and 25% of the total transit revenue passengers (surface plus rapid transit). Therefore, the author excluded New York City from his field case studies because of its unique scale of operation. The conclusions and recommendations of this study may thus not necessarily be applicable to transit operations in smaller cities, or to the New York City Transit Authority.

An analysis of patronage and financial data has shown that the industry is experiencing the pressures of a secularly declining demand (although the demand for rapid transit in some cities has leveled off or increased slightly), intensification of the peak-load problem, rising fares, and increased operating expenses. As a result profit margins are almost nonexistent among the larger transit companies. In 1961 the total cash flow (profit plus depreciation) of the twelve companies studied (representing 61%

of the industry's gross investment) was approximately $13 million. Yet two recent estimates indicate that the industry will need at least $10 billion during the next two decades for modernization and expansion. If these forecasts are accurate, it is clear that the $375 million federal aid to mass transit program voted in the summer of 1964 will cover only a small portion of the industry's future needs.

Within this general pattern of economic distress the evidence shows that in 1961 the average operating ratio (operating expense excluding depreciation and fixed charges divided by revenue) of the five private companies in the sample was more favorable than for the remaining seven public companies. It is interesting to note that rapid transit operations alone did not imply either high or low operating ratios. Although New York City, Chicago, and Boston tended to have high operating ratios, Philadelphia and Cleveland had relatively favorable operating ratios in 1961.

As discussed in Chapter 2, this study made no effort to consider in depth the reasons for this difference in performance, although the author suggested that the major variables would include price policies, political pressures, and the ability to control labor costs. This subject might well warrant close study during the next decade, for the transition from private to public ownership will continue, either because of financial distress, or because communities object to the fare increases, dividend payments, and pleas for tax reduction of the solvent private companies.

External Pressures Confronting Mass Transit

There is no denying that external pressures (such as population density, automobile ownership and use, central city development) have been major factors in the secular decline of transit patronage. Indeed, the author's questionnaire revealed that many executives in the transit industry believe that external factors beyond their control constitute the industry's greatest problem.

The author has concluded, however, that there have been shifts relatively favorable to transit in these external pressures, including the following: (1) Serious efforts are now being made by the federal, state, and local governments to redevelop our central cities and central business districts. As noted in Chapter 2, transit's fate rests largely on CBD and central city traffic. (2) The urban highway program is encountering stiff resistance in some areas with many persons calling for balanced highway and transit systems. (3) The federal government, for the first time, is now providing financial aid for the transit industry. (4) The 1962 favorable referendum vote for a $1 billion rapid transit system in San Francisco may be an indication of grass roots support for transit. (5) In 1964 Massachusetts became the first state to enact legislation providing state tax revenue for transit projects.

In view of these changes in the external environment, the internal strategies of mass transit management take on added importance. In the opinion of the author, the industry can no longer claim that factors beyond its control leave transit executives powerless in the struggle to regain riders.

Internal Strategies of Transit Management

A strategy has been defined by the author as a set of policies keyed to specific objectives. In addition to the daily task of maintaining and dispatching hundreds of vehicles in our largest cities, transit management encounters major problems in other internal strategy areas. The industry is only beginning to emerge from an almost nonexistent research and development program. Historically, research and development activity was limited because of lack of interest by the industry's suppliers plus a shortage of funds and personnel within the transit industry. The author's questionnaire and interviews disclosed a major problem in recruiting future management personnel. At the same time, many transit companies have failed to institute programs to develop managerial talent within the organization.

The economic decline of the industry has produced a severe labor relations problem. This issue promises to grow in severity, for the industry is labor rather than capital intensive, and in the face of present trends it cannot depend upon traffic and revenue growth to cover the costs of increased pay and more favorable working conditions. In addition, the interviews, questionnaire, and statistical data suggest that as the industry continues its transition from private to public enterprise, these labor pressures will increase, for some politicians, anxious to obtain votes, tend to side with labor in its demands. Of course, the introduction of automation could theoretically reduce future labor costs. Automation at present, however, seems limited to a few rapid transit routes, and it also will be subject to labor and political pressures.

In short, it is understandable that management emphasizes the labor problem. But, in the opinion of the author, the more important task facing transit management is to stimulate demand to produce increased revenues to meet the secularly rising costs. Thus, the author has concluded that marketing assumes major importance in the priority of management's internal strategies, for as Figure 3.1 indicates, it alone directly attempts to stimulate the consumer demand for transit service.

The Results of Marketing Strategy: Patronage and Profitability

The evidence used in analyzing management's marketing practices has consisted of field case studies of expressway bus lines, rapid transit operations, suburban plant bus service, and senior citizen fares, a questionnaire, and the literature. The case studies were developed with the objective of reporting and analyzing the more significant attempts to market urban mass transit in the cities the author visited. The findings of this study constitute the results of a broad variety of management marketing strategies.

Patronage

In general the evidence indicates that patronage on both the expressway bus routes and rapid transit increased sharply during an initial one- to two-year period, but then either continued to increase at a significantly reduced rate or began to decline in common with the company's over-all patronage trend.[1] Although the rail rapid transit routes carried impressive numbers of riders

---

[1] See Tables 2.2 (Cleveland Rapid), 5.1, and 6.2. Cleveland's growth was in two stages: 1955–1957, and following the extension to West Park in 1958, 1958–1960.

(in terms of equivalent automobiles) on a scale far greater than those of any of the express bus lines, several of the routes were operating at substantially less than track capacity.[2] In addition, traffic studies suggested that substantial numbers of automobile drivers in each of the rapid transit cities were making the kinds of trips that the rapid transit routes could serve.

The two suburban industrial plant bus services (Chapter 4) showed relatively low patronage, approximately 120 to 130 trips per plant per day. This would be the equivalent of about one full busload in each direction. On the other hand, the senior citizen fare plan in Los Angeles (Chapter 4) increased patronage 24% to a level of slightly over 10 million rides per year.

Perhaps the most interesting patronage statistics were the percentage of new riders diverted from automobiles. The best example was the express bus service in Los Angeles, where the direct, comfortable, fast (within the limitations of expressway congestion) service produced a diversion factor of 60%. The percentages of new rapid transit riders diverted from automobiles were substantially lower, even though the absolute figures were more impressive. On the outer half of Boston's Highland Branch, 37% of the riders formerly used automobiles. This percentage dropped to 30% at two outer rapid transit stations in Cleveland, and 11.5% on the whole of the Congress Street rapid transit line in Chicago.

Profitability

It has been more difficult for the author to develop conclusions with respect to the profitability of bus and rapid transit operations because of difficulties in revenue and overhead cost allocation. He has concluded from the available evidence that each of the express bus operations covered its minimum out-of-pocket costs, its overhead expenses (except for possibly Chicago), and in addition, in Philadelphia, depreciation and fixed charges. But none of the bus routes could be termed a "heavy" profit maker. Likewise, three of the four rapid transit lines covered their out-

---

[2] See Tables 5.1 and 6.2. Peak-hour bus loads ranged from 386 to 812 persons. Rapid transit peak-hour patronage varied from 1,527 to 18,000 riders.

of-pocket and overhead expenses and contributed to the system's depreciation and fixed charges. The exception was Boston's Highland Branch rapid transit line, which suffered both an operating and a capital deficit in 1960 despite heavy patronage because of an abnormally low fare structure and high operating costs.

It should be noted that this profitability experience contrasts sharply with the performance of eastern commuter railroads, which continue to experience both operating and capital deficits. Thus, it might be preferable on the basis of financial performance for urban areas to concentrate their efforts in promoting rail transportation via rapid transit rather than commuter railroads.

The suburban industrial plant bus experiences in Chicago and Cleveland indicate that this type of operation cannot be operated at a profit unless the plant is located at the natural terminal of a central business district trunk line. The Los Angeles off-peak-hour senior citizen fare plan revealed that patronage could be stimulated with a fare reduction, but that the company might suffer a slight loss in annual revenues. It is also possible that the revenue decrease might have been offset by faster vehicle operation because of shifts in patronage from the peak hours.

An Evaluation of Management's Marketing Strategy

A major objective of this study has been to report and analyze the strengths and weaknesses in transit management's marketing strategy. The author has defined the elements of an integrated marketing strategy to include market research, pricing, product planning, and promotional policies. Each element plays a vital role. Market research identifies a segment of the urban travel market which mass transit can serve. Product planning decisions dictate the quality of the service which will be offered. The service is then priced and promoted to the public.

In general, the author has concluded that there were some significant weaknesses in the companies' marketing strategies. These included poor product planning, the unwillingness to invest in market research and extensive promotion, and the failure to integrate rapid transit product planning and pricing to create a high quality service at a high price which would appeal to the more affluent segments of the traveling public. In short, the cases showed no example of a completely integrated marketing strategy keyed toward differentiated segments of the urban travel market. On the other hand, there were many individual instances of well-thought-out and implemented policies, particularly in the marketing of express bus service. These conclusions will be amplified in the following sections under the headings of the policy components of marketing strategy: pricing, market research, promotion, and product planning.

Price Policy

Pricing remains one of the key elements in marketing strategy because of its direct impact on profits and utilization of capacity. The cases have shown a wide diversity in approaches to pricing, and the author has grouped his conclusions into the categories of the level of the rate, changes in the rate, and method of collection.

There is ample evidence to support the conclusion that the level of the fare is critical, if the transit marketing package is to be both attractive and cover operating expenses. For example, in cases of bus or PCC streetcar operation (both characterized by relatively unfavorable ratios of seat-labor cost) nonstop express service must be accompanied by a premium fare to offset partially the lack of passenger turnover en route. Likewise a trade-off can be made between standing loads and a low fare or seats-for-all and a high fare. Most companies have now recognized that long routes require a zone fare to break even, even though there may be difficulties in collecting the zone fare. Although transit has always preferred the flat systemwide fare because of ease of collection, it seems reasonable to conclude that fare structures will have to become more complex as trade-offs are made among fare, standards of comfort, and speed on perhaps a route-by-route basis.

In addition, the evidence also suggests that the historical surcharges for transfers or parking fees in connection with rapid transit may deter riders. Thus, pricing policy must also take into consideration the possibility of lost round-trip base fares versus the incremental revenues from surcharges.

At times during his research, the author had the feeling that not enough attention was being given to the implications of changes in existing rates. For example, many officials tended to regard the elasticity factor of .33 (Simpson & Curtin formula) as "given," regardless of the class of rider subject to the fare change. Yet the Los Angeles senior citizen fare experience showed much smaller revenue losses than would have been forecast by the Simpson & Curtin formula. Thus, although the Simpson & Curtin formula may yield accurate results on a systemwide basis, it does not appear to be as useful in predicting results of fare changes on individual routes because of the different classes of riders.

But perhaps the most significant change in price policy may hinge on the method of collection rather than the rate of fare. The senior citizen plan suggests that identification cards can be used to prevent abuse, a major reason why transit executives have abandoned the pass. Indeed, as discussed in Chapter 4, the pass or validation card might lead to credit billing, integrated into a data processing system which would yield data on origins and destination, load factors, elasticities of demand, and other data vital for adjusting management marketing strategy.

Market Research Policy

Chapter 3 indicated the dynamic changes in land use in our urban communities. As a result the patterns of demand for transit service are changing constantly. The task of market research is to monitor existing and potential demand for transit and to recommend changes in transit service to attract riders.

The cases show both strengths and weaknesses in the marketing research effort. On the positive side were Cleveland's use of punched card tabulating equipment to plan a bus service, Los Angeles' questionnaire survey of senior citizen riders, and the use of census data in Cleveland, Philadelphia, and Chicago to plan bus and rapid transit routes.

Yet the author felt that too much effort was being devoted to maintaining descriptive historical tabulations of persons riding transit, rather than finding out who was not riding transit and why. In addition, relatively few postcard surveys were taken of existing transit riders to find answers to important questions such as previous mode of travel, reason for trip, etc. There seemed to be a general reluctance to use sampling techniques (an important exception was the aforementioned senior citizen questionnaire) to obtain this market research type of data. Indeed, several officials expressed skepticism of "3%" samples which formed the basis of regional transportation studies being undertaken throughout the nation.

Much of the problem stems from the fact that the transit industry employs relatively few persons skilled in market research. In turn, coordination with urban planning groups is hampered by the fact that not enough men in the industry speak "the same language" as the urban planners. This apparent lack of coordination is particularly regrettable, inasmuch as these urban studies can theoretically provide valuable origin-destination data for the transit industry.

Promotion Policy

Despite severe budget limitations, the promotional campaigns accompanying most of the new services discussed in the cases were good. In particular, the "kick-off" campaigns in the rapid transit cases (complete with pamphlets, advertising, speeches, free rides, etc.) accomplished the objective of making the public aware of the new service. In the author's opinion, an outstanding component of the promotional policy in all of the express bus cases and most of the rapid transit operations was the use of timetables to inform the public as to the times of departure, running times, route, and rates of fare of each of the lines.

The author also believes, however, that there were some weaknesses in the promotional campaigns. Many of the companies expected the potential or actual rider to write in for timetables or pick them up in stations or on vehicles. Even Cleveland, with its excellent program of mailing timetables seasonally to 100,000 homes, depended on the consumer to put his name on its list. In view of the continuing shifts of population in residential areas, it seems reasonable to conclude that the transit industry may be forced in many instances to take a more aggressive approach to promotion. Yet a successful promotional campaign still is dependent on the attractiveness of the product. It is indeed a waste of funds and energy to try to convince the public that a bad product is "Jet Age" transportation.

Product Planning Policy

In this study the analysis has focused on decisions concerning speed, comfort, and convenience as a part of the transit marketing package. It is significant to compare the differences in policy in the expressway bus and rapid transit cases. Three of the four express bus routes featured seats-for-all, nonstop express portions of the route (which segregated short-and long-haul passengers and speeded the ride) and direct one-vehicle suburban-CBD service. Each of these factors differentiated the express bus service from the typical transit trip.

On the other hand, each of the "Jet Age" rapid transit routes carried substantial numbers of standees during the peak hours. In addition, two of the four companies declined to operate express trains with the result that the average terminal-to-terminal speeds were below 23 mph. In contrast, Cleveland's general manager insisted on nonstop express service on its double track West Side rapid transit route, and the evidence indicates that the express trains have been extremely popular. Thus, in several instances the new rapid transit routes have failed to produce significant improvements in the standards of speed or comfort over existing rapid transit lines.

Another significant contrast between the express bus and rapid transit policies was the question of parking lots. None of the bus routes attempted to attract riders from beyond the immediate service area of the bus line, yet 47% of the riders on Los Angeles' West Valley Freeway Flyer reached the bus route by automobile. In contrast, each of the rapid transit lines provided parking lots, and the evidence indicates that some lots were popular even in areas of low population density (for example, Cleveland). But the Boston case showed that fare increases plus poor standards of speed and comfort could result in unused parking lot capacity.

Perhaps the most important weakness in the product planning was the failure of any of the cities to adopt air conditioning. It seems to the author that air conditioning is the most inexpensive way for transit to change its "image" from that of a cheap, uncomfortable method of transportation to a modern component of our urban transportation network. Yet the questionnaire revealed a reluctance on the part of management to air condition 100% of its vehicles, even if funds were available. The author suggests that this response confirmed the tendency of transit management to invest in projects which make the production task easier in contrast to investments in marketing *per se*.

It must be re-emphasized that the recent ordering of air-conditioned rapid transit cars by the Chicago Transit Authority and Port of New York Authority, plus the purchase of air-conditioned buses by Pittsburgh's Allegheny County Port Authority, may be an indication of a major shift in management attitudes between 1962 and 1964. Likewise, the San Francisco Bay Area Rapid Transit District has promised that its fast, comfortable, seats-for-all, rapid transit cars will be air conditioned. On the other hand, the New York City Transit Authority labeled its new 1964 World's Fair equipment the "most modern today," even though the cars were not air conditioned.

The author's questionnaire plus data in the trade literature indicate that the mass transit industry and many transportation experts favor rail rapid transit as the major component of public transportation systems in our largest cities. It seems logical, therefore, that transit management would concentrate relatively more of its marketing efforts on rapid transit. Perhaps the most important conclusion of this study is that the opposite has been the case, for the marketing decisions in the rapid transit cases have been markedly inferior to those in the other cited cases.

In short, management's task appears to be to plan and implement integrated marketing strategies keyed to the varying requirements of its customers. To a certain extent this was done in the development of the expressway and suburban plant bus services and the senior citizen fare plan. But these marketing considerations were often conspicuously absent in the rapid transit cases. The immediate challenge to management will be to improve the marketing of its rapid transit service; the ultimate objective, however, should be to develop an over-all plan for marketing the full range of transit service. The final comments on this point will be reserved for the recommendations at the end of the chapter.

The Interrelationship Between Marketing and Political Strategy

In Chapter 4 the analysis of the literature, questionnaire, and field interviews suggested that the transition from private to public enterprise would intensify the traditional problems between the transit industry and agencies of the government and that marketing strategy could help reinforce political strategy. The case studies in Chapter 5 and 6 provide data to confirm these observations.

Each of the companies, both public and private (Philadelphia), failed to obtain financing for critical features of the rapid transit marketing package including sufficient equipment, modern stations (platform lengths and escalators), parking lots, express tracks, or CBD distribution, with the result that the marketing task of transit management was made much more difficult.

The reasons for these failures included (1) personal antagonism between public and transit officials, (2) disagreements between public and transit officials on the role of the transit company (e.g., should it be serving the suburbs or low-income central city residents without access to an automobile?), or (3) the inability or unwillingness of the governmental unit to spend additional funds on the transit project.

The last observation may well be the most significant. As noted in Chapter 6, reporters in each of the cities mentioned to the author that "the man in the street" is either apathetic or dislikes the transit company intensely. Thus, it is not surprising that the transit company finds it difficult to obtain political support for its projects. In addition, the field trips disclosed strong political interest groups promoting the automobiles and highways. These groups included planners, public officials, and businessmen.

The business community cannot be expected to endorse transit unanimously. Many firms have abandoned locations in the central cities to locate in the suburbs. Others maintain some central city activity but are increasing their investments in the suburbs. In urban areas which are not experiencing over-all growth, policies which promote the central business district must do so at the expense of established enterprises in suburbia. Also, politicians representing the suburbs are not inclined to support activities benefiting the central city, particularly if suburban taxes are increased. Finally, as noted in Chapters 1 and 3, the planners are not wholly convinced that mass transportation is vital. Therefore, mass transit aid which most directly benefits the central cities and central business districts is not easy to obtain.

In view of the above observations, the interrelationship between marketing and political strategy becomes apparent, for the traditional stigma of mass transit (dirty, slow, uncomfortable, unpleasant) must be replaced with an "image" of progress and modernity. The Philadelphia Transportation Company's success in convincing the regulatory commission to approve its express bus operation may well have been tied to the support of the residents served by the area and the downtown business community. This support hinged largely on the proposed marketing package; favorable rates, direct and fast route, seats-for-all, and all-day service. On the other hand, until very recently the mass transportation industry has experienced great difficulty in obtaining political support for rapid transit extensions. It seems reasonable to conclude that the public is not impressed by statements that rapid transit has the capacity to carry 40,000 passengers per hour if it means 40,000 persons packed into slow, uncomfortable vehicles. Again, the success of the San Francisco Bay Area Rapid Transit District in obtaining funds may well lie in its intensive promotion of a new, modern rapid transit image.

Formal Organization

A major conclusion of this study pertains to the formal organization of companies in the transit industry. The cases have shown that a transit company is organized by function, primarily to delegate authority and responsibility for production-oriented tasks (e.g., driving and maintaining the vehicles). Staff support for these production activities is provided by the public relations, engineering, planning, comptroller, and legal departments.

What is lacking is a marketing-oriented group, which is organized by either product (such as director of commuter service) or project (for example, rapid transit project director). The problem of formal organization is particularly acute in the case of rapid transit, for, in contrast, the small scale of express bus operations allows "informal" monitoring of their operations by one of the functional officials. Yet in no company was one individual below the general manager assigned continuing formal responsibility for marketing rapid transit, and the questionnaire further indicated that most of the transit executives spent relatively little time on marketing problems.

The author believes that this failure to assign continuing marketing responsibility may well account for much of the weakness in marketing strategy mentioned above. Under the present functional organization, the only official who continually represents the marketing point of view is the director of public relations, and judging from the size of his budget appropriation, his position is not too strong.

Recommendations

Urban Planners

At the present time our largest cities are entering a period when major policy decisions with respect to land use will have to be made. In each of the cities visited by the author—Cleveland, Chicago, Boston, Philadelphia, and even Los Angeles (the archtype of urban sprawl according to some)—extensive demolition has taken place in the central cities and central business districts. Ironically, urban renewal will hurt mass transit in the short run, for between the start of demolition and the end of new construction years of inactive land use may pass. But if in the long run urban renewal should succeed in revitalizing the blighted sections of our urban areas, and make the central city a better place to work, shop, and live, the future for urban mass transit may be bright.

As noted in Chapter 3, there is a great deal of controversy over the appropriate land use patterns for urban communities and the role that transit should play in the handling of trip demands within urban regions. In the author's opinion, the challenge to transit management is to make its service attractive enough that the planners, political officials, and the public will demand transit facilities in addition to highways and parking lots to serve the redeveloped cities.

The author recommends specifically to urban planners that they should reserve judgment on rapid transit's ability to divert automobile drivers until at least one modern route is built embodying the standards of speed and comfort discussed previously. It seems unfair to develop generalizations as to consumer attitudes toward rapid mass transit when, in fact, most persons have never been exposed to a modern rapid transit system.

The cases also suggest that particular attention should be paid to the design components of a modern mass transit system. Rights of way must be wide enough for express tracks or bus lanes, for it is apparent that speed is one of the major factors which attracts persons to mass transit. The design of the central business district should provide for traffic-free mass transit distribution to maximize transit's average speed. Finally, suburban parking lots at the ends of bus or rapid transit routes should be carefully designed to avoid traffic congestion, which conceivably could be as serious as congestion on expressways if the volumes of patronage hoped for by the transit industry should materialize.

Public Administrators

The conclusions reached in this study clearly indicate that the decisions of public policy can have an important impact on the success of marketing strategy, both in the stages of initial design and finance and in day-to-day operation. The author's recommendations are grouped under the familiar headings used throughout this study: promotion, regulation, and pressure.

If public administrators want intensive land use in our central cities, it seems appropriate to suggest that they work actively to promote modern mass transit. This will require both a willingness to provide capital aid (at the local, state, and federal levels) and approval of design features sufficient to attract suburban as well as central city patronage to rapid transit.

Although the problems of regulation are fast disappearing as the transit industry moves from private to public enterprise, there has been a tendency for informal pressures to replace formal regulation on issues such as fare increases. Therefore, political administrators can provide significant assistance to the industry by either agreeing on a well-defined policy of either capital and/or operating subsidies or accepting the inevitable fare increases necessary for solvent operation.

The final task of political administrators would appear to be to help insure that the transit company remains free from undue political or labor pressures. Specifically, appointments to executive boards (in public companies) must be qualified and nonpartisan to insure sound and consistent transit policies, as well as to prevent frictions between the board and career officials. Similarly, continual efforts must be made to protect the transit company from patronage pressures at the lower levels, for, as has been noted, the failure to control labor costs in this labor-intensive industry can lead only to demoralization of the staff and continual deficits.

Transit Industry

Marketing Strategy: The recommendations concerning marketing strategy follow from the conclusions outlined earlier in this chapter. The basic marketing problem of mass transit is to provide a service which is more attractive to the consumer than his automobile. For many segments of the population, particularly those living in suburbia, the quality of the service appears to be more important than the price. Therefore, the author recommends that: (1) immediate steps be taken to improve the quality of transit service by air conditioning its equipment, and (2) transit management plan integrated marketing strategies, not around the concept of mass transportation, but rather around a series of marketing packages designed to attract different classes of riders.

Air conditioning appears to be the quickest and least costly means of changing the image of mass transit. An immediate policy should be that in cities where service industries such as restaurants and movies are normally air conditioned, all future equipment will be air conditioned. As noted in Chapter 6, the incremental costs of air conditioning, especially on rapid transit cars, will be small. At the same time, it might be well to evaluate the costs of air conditioning existing equipment versus the undeniable benefits.

The transit marketing packages would reflect a series of consistent market research, product planning, pricing, and promotion policies, thereby constituting truly integrated marketing strategies. At the outset, the transit industry will have to support the concept of market research by recruiting persons trained in this function and encouraging greater cooperation between transit companies and regional planners. One outgrowth of such research would be "tailored commuter service." Surveys of business firms along major routes, processed on mechanical or electronic equipment, would indicate cluster points of potential riders (in time and space). During the afternoon rush hour many outbound buses would display "No Passenger" signs and proceed to the indicated "cluster points." As workers emerged from buildings, the buses would be waiting, much in the same manner as transit companies presently handle special school bus trips. This kind of service would overcome a major handicap of surface bus scheduling, whereby once a vehicle leaves its terminal it continues unsupervised until the end of the line. As a result, because of traffic delays, vehicles bunch up with some buses running filled and others half empty. By keeping buses stationary at cluster points until they are filled, surface capacity can be better utilized.

A major element in the marketing package would be a variety of "products" geared to the requirements of different riders. Product planning would be coordinated with price policies to insure profitable operation. At one end of the spectrum would be a high quality service from suburban parking lots to the central business district. The critical product planning policies would include seats-for-all, air conditioning, nonstop express service between suburbia and the CBD, and all-day operation. A premium fare would be required to offset the seats-for-all policy as well as the impossibility of passenger turnover on nonstop express service. The nonstop express service would also segregate long- and short-haul passengers and perhaps attract those suburban-CBD travelers who may not want to travel in the company of less affluent members of the urban community.

It appears significant to the author that Los Angeles' Freeway Flyer came closest to meeting the specifications of the suburbia-CBD high quality marketing package. As previously noted, 60% of the Freeway Flyer's patronage formerly used automobiles, despite the lack of air-conditioned bus equipment and freeway congestion which restricted operating speeds. Although the Freeway Flyer did not charge a premium fare, the standard Los Angeles zone fare enabled the operation to cover expenses.

On the other hand, this kind of high quality-high priced package was conspicuously absent in the rapid transit cases. If the transit industry is to generate support in the suburbs for rapid transit extensions, it appears essential that it offer a similar marketing package to the suburban communities. A plan for this kind of service, embodying the trade-off between product planning and pricing, was outlined in Chapter 6 using the Congress line in Chicago as an example. It is interesting to note that the San Francisco Bay Area Transit District promises many of the elements, particularly air conditioning and seats-for-all. Rather than wait until 1970 for the full operation in San Francisco, the transit industry might well utilize part of the 1964 $375 million federal mass transportation aid program to inaugurate premium quality rapid transit service immediately in other cities to bolster its image.

In the middle of the quality-price spectrum would be the existing forms of bus or rapid transit service. Although traditional loading standards would be maintained, air conditioning and better scheduling, such as "tailored commuter service," should make transit more attractive.

At the lower end of the spectrum would be a low fare, spartan service for school children. During peak hours special equipment would be operated on regular routes for school riders. All other vehicles would charge the full adult fare for all classes of riders. Such service would improve standards of comfort for adult passengers, and segregate revenues and costs of school bus operations to permit the determination of the economics of school bus service.

The final element of an integrated marketing strategy would be promotion. Timetables would be placed at bus stops and rapid transit stations, and a personalized promotion campaign which mailed timetables to riders could reinforce the improvements in service. It might be possible to minimize expenses by coordinating this type of program with department store or public utility mailings. In the event that the transit industry adopts credit cards and periodic billings, this kind of promotional campaign would be relatively easy to administer.

Political Strategy: The following recommendations are not meant to constitute an over-all program of political strategy. For example, this study did not consider in detail techniques of legislative or executive access, the question of supporting political candidates, or the skills required to draft legislation so as to appeal to a variety of interest groups. Rather, the recommendations indicate areas in which marketing and political strategy can reinforce each other.

The first set of recommendations is directed to the industry as a whole and follows from the analysis of efforts to obtain government promotion at the federal level as discussed in Chapter 4. If the industry is to continue to obtain during the next two decades the substantial amount of capital it needs to modernize and expand, it would appear that there must be internal agreement on the type of aid wanted; the industry must supply useful information to the executive and legislative sectors of the government as to the costs and benefits of mass transit; and perhaps most important, the industry must implement marketing strategies which will produce tangible results from existing aid programs.

The second set of recommendations is company, rather than industry, oriented. In the fight for government promotion, fair regulation, and minimization of political pressure, the transit company's political strategy must be supported by special interest groups and the general public. Examples of the former include urban planners, downtown businessmen, neighborhood civic groups, suppliers to the industry, regional public officials, organizations representing those who cannot drive automobiles (such as senior citizens or school children), and representatives of those suburban communities which have a strong interest in the economic health of the central city.

The support of special interest groups will best be cultivated by a carefully planned program of supplying relevant information. The information would be keyed to each particular interest group. For example, when speaking to urban planners vague generalities such as "one transit lane is worth thirty automobile lanes" should be avoided. In its place would be the detailed costs and benefits of moving observed volumes of traffic by different modes between selected origins and destinations. Presentations to neighborhood civic groups would emphasize the costs of different levels of transit service or the problems in transporting school children. The chamber of commerce could be periodically briefed on transit revenues, expenses, worker productivity, correlations with indicators of economic activity, and operating performance versus transit systems in other cities, thereby enhancing the transit company's image as a well-run business and generating support against legislative interference and patronage.

In addition, the transit industry can secure broad public support, as suggested previously, by improving its company marketing "image." A senior citizen fare might lead to political support, whereas service cuts just before an election could spell defeat of a legislative program. Most important, the marketing strategies should reflect the differing requirements of the general public. Thus, at the risk of repetition, a "one city-one fare" policy may be quite inappropriate, for many segments of the population will be willing to pay premium fares for premium service. Likewise standing-room-only rapid transit service at low cost may be acceptable to certain income groups, but quite distasteful to the growing mass market of suburbia.

These product planning and pricing policies can be reinforced by a personalized promotional program in conjunction with timetable mailings. Brochures could be used to inform the community on public policy questions affecting transit. The public may feel more disposed to vote "yes" on transit referenda if it feels that the transit company is taking a personal interest in each voter.

Finally, it might be wise to appoint a man or group skilled in political strategy to provide staff assistance to the executive board or chief administrative officer on questions of political strategy, rather than lumping such activities under the heading of public relations or the legal department.

Formal Organization: Throughout this study, the author has emphasized that the marketing and political strategies can be a by-product of the orientation of the company. If the company is organized primarily to produce rather than sell its service, it is likely to lose touch with the needs and wants of the consumer. In the author's opinion, the transit industry falls into this category.

Figure 7.1 presents a modification of Cleveland's formal organization chart (chosen for illustrative purposes only; see Chapter 2, Figure 2.2) which delegates formal responsibility and authority for marketing and political strategies in the same manner that the existing organization provides for the planning and day-to-day implementation of production-oriented activities. Of course there can be variations in this general theme of organizing to sell as well as produce the product. Some alternatives will be mentioned in connection with the following discussion of several of the titles shown on the chart.

(1) Manager of Marketing—This key official would bring to top management a continuing concern for the consumer and the coordinated marketing task. In staff meetings with the general manager he would state the case for investing in market research, promotion, or improved product planning. He would be expected to support his proposals with financial data and counter arguments from the production-oriented officials, such as manager of maintenance and manager of operations. It would seem appropriate that the manager of marketing know the problems of the operating departments yet maintain a "marketing orientation" if his group is to be effective. He would also serve as a major coordinating official with representatives of the Housing and Home Finance Agency (HHFA) in connection with capital grants or demonstration projects.

releases and articles for publications, and in conjunction with the directors of governmental affairs and promotion, plan and implement grass roots political strategy. As noted previously, public relations could be transferred under the manager of marketing; however, the author prefers to keep its activities separate, primarily to insure that at least two individuals—the managers of marketing and public relations—would bring the "marketing orientation" to staff meetings.

(8) Governmental Affairs—The director of governmental affairs would head up a staff group responsible for advising the general manager and executive board on questions of public policy, carrying on lobbying and educational campaigns designed to inform public administrators and coordinate with the promotion and public relations staffs on questions of grass roots campaigns.

It is obvious that the recommended changes in formal organization may require hiring more personnel. On the one hand, though, many within the existing organization could be transferred to new positions (e.g., members of the schedule department shifted under the manager of marketing). Only their orientation would change from that of production and costs to one of marketing, patronage, revenues, and profits.

On the other hand, even if the staff should have to be enlarged, it would appear that the investment would be worthwhile for two reasons. The pay-off could be substantial if the marketing group succeeds in attracting both riders and capital aid. The product or project emphasis of the recommended formal organization would provide excellent interfaces with the HHFA capital aid and demonstration programs. Also the new openings in marketing and political affairs might attract future managerial talent from colleges and graduate schools into the transit industry, thus alleviating the critical problem of recruitment.

Although the transit industry is beset by powerful external pressures, management has the power to adjust marketing and political strategies, and particularly the formal organization. If the organization reflects a balance between production and marketing, it is not unreasonable to forecast more effective marketing strategies.

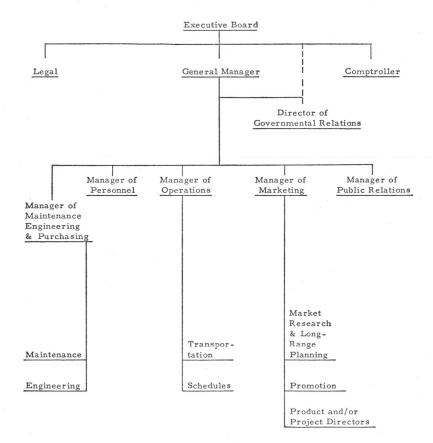

Figure 7.1

A Proposal for Formal Organization of a Transit Company

(2) Market Research and Long-Range Planning—This group would concentrate on questions of long-range planning in conjunction with urban redevelopment, new rapid transit and surface routes, and the highway program, and coordinate with transportation study groups at the city, state, or federal levels. It would include engineers and market research technicians and provide staff assistance when required by others in the marketing group.

(3) Promotion—The author recommends that the promotion function be removed from under the existing director of public relations to focus on advertising and a continuing program of timetable distribution. In short, it would be responsible for the first objective of a promotional campaign to inform actual and potential riders of the speed, time of departure, and price of existing service. Some companies might prefer to continue to have the director of public relations responsible for promotion. In such cases it might be better to bring both the public relations and promotional departments under the manager of marketing.

(4) Product and/or Project Directors—Continuing responsibility for planning and implementing marketing strategies for transit routes would be delegated to product or project directors and their staffs. Some companies might prefer to organize the groups by product responsibility, such as directors of commuter or off-peak services, whereas other firms would assign project responsibility; for example, directors of rapid transit, surface lines, or tours and charter services. There is no reason that both product and project responsibility could not be delegated, for example, with a director of commuter operations coordinating with directors of surface and rapid transit lines.

These groups would be responsible for monitoring patronage, revenue, and profit trends of individual routes; determining "share of the market" of important lines (such as rapid transit); evaluating the "price-product planning" trade-off of each route; setting patronage and profit targets of important lines and services; coordinating with the market research and planning group on new rapid transit and surface routes and services; coordinating with the public relations department in answering customer

complaints; and making recommendations to the manager of marketing on the pricing and product planning components of marketing strategy. In connection with the last function, the product or project directors would take over from the schedule department the responsibility for determining demand on each route and also would recommend loading standards and types of service to the general manager through the manager of marketing. Thus, the product and project directors together with the manager of marketing would be responsible for planning and selling marketing packages to the organization. It should be noted that the effectiveness of the marketing group will depend upon the willingness of the general manager to adopt their suggestions. If their recommendations are continually vetoed by the operating departments, the company will be unable to achieve the needed balance between production and marketing.

(5) Schedules—as noted above, the schedule department would relinquish its function of determining demand, but would continue to produce a production plan consistent with the labor agreement, vehicle availability, standards of speed and comfort proposed by the product or project directors and approved by the general manager, and demand characteristics for each route supplied by the product or project directors. Hopefully, the schedule department will succeed in converting most of the manual scheduling procedures to electronic data processing. The author has chosen to keep the schedule department under the operations manager to signify its continuing production orientation. However, the department could also logically be transferred under the manager of marketing.

(6) Transportation—This production-oriented line group would continue to perform its task of dispatching and controlling the vehicles according to the day-to-day plan supplied by the schedule department.

(7) Public Relations—The author recommends that the public relations staff concentrate on questions of public relations rather than both public relations and promotion. The office would serve as a clearing house for complaints (much of which would be routed to either the product or project directors), handle press

The challenge to management to make changes in its existing practices seems critical at the present time. For it appears that its marketing strategies will largely determine whether the industry enjoys a renaissance marked by modernization and growth, or whether it takes a final plunge to the status of an unpleasant tax-supported public service, providing spartan, cheap transportation (primarily for those who cannot drive) in urban communities designed for and dominated by the private automobile.

APPENDIX
Questionnaire

1. My efforts as chief administrative officer are devoted to: (Please indicate what percentage of your time is devoted to the following problems)
   a. Operating (including labor)   _____%
   b. Financial   _____%
   c. Legal (including claims)   _____%
   d. Marketing (including public relations)   _____%
   e. Engineering   _____%
   f. Other _____   _____%

2. Please rank the following in order of importance:
   I personally believe that the critical problems facing urban mass transportation are:
   ( ) Declining demand for the service caused by factors beyond the control of management (e.g., expansion of residential and industrial activity in the suburbs)
   ( ) Rising labor costs
   ( ) Inability to finance capital improvements
   ( ) Failure of technology to develop a mass transit vehicle which can divert the public from the private automobile
   ( ) Inequitable government policies (e.g., federal promotion and financing of express highways)
   ( ) Lack of dynamic, trained personnel rising up through management in the urban mass transit industry

3. Please answer each of the following *either* (1) Rise 10% or more; (2) Fall 10% or more; or (3) Remain within 10% of present levels:
   During the next five years, I expect that on our system:
   a. Revenue passengers will   ( )
   b. Passenger revenues will   ( )
   c. Charter and special service revenues   ( )
   d. Net operating income (revenues less operating expenses)   ( )
   e. Net income   ( )

4. Executive Profile Data Sheet

Data Category	Board of Directors or Trustees	Chief Administrative Officer	Supt. of Transportation or Operations Manager	Treasurer Comptroller	Chief Engineer
1. Age: (high, low, and average for Board)*					
2. Experience in transit industry (number of years, high, low, and average for Board)					
3. Was this individual's previous job *within* or *outside* the company?	Leave Blank				
If from *within*, what was his previous job title?	Leave Blank				

If from *outside*, how was the individual recruited? Choose: Leave Blank

  A. Political
  B. Consultant's recommendation
  C. Personal contact
  D. National reputation

When this position *next* becomes vacant, from which of the above will the successor *most likely* come?   Leave Blank

4. Highest educational level of *present* holder of the position   Leave Blank

5. Most likely educational level of *next* person to fill position   Leave Blank

* Thus, if there is a five-man Board with ages of 60, 58, 55, 42, and 35; enter 60–35–50.0 in the space.

NOTE: THESE DATA AS WELL AS ALL OTHER DATA IN THIS QUESTIONNAIRE WILL BE USED SO AS TO NOT REVEAL THE PARTICIPATING OFFICIALS OR THEIR COMPANIES.

5. The following job titles in our company are responsible to the chief administrative officer for policies in the following areas:
   (e.g., revenue accounting *comptroller*)
   Fare strategy
   New equipment purchases   _____
   New routes   _____
   Changes in service (e.g., express service)   _____
   Labor relations   _____
   Market research   _____
   Coordination with regional planning agency   _____
   Coordination with city on operating problems   _____
   Recruitment of management personnel and
      management training   _____

6. Please answer each of the following Yes or No.
   1. Our company has an active management recruiting program.   _____
   2. Our company has a formal management training program.   _____
   3. The typical member of our management training program has a college education.   _____
   4. A young man graduating from college can look forward to a satisfying career in urban mass transportation.   _____
   5. In comparison with other occupations, members of the management team are well paid.   _____

7. What percentage of your expenses normally goes to advertising and public relations? _____
   Is this class of expense: (choose *one*)
   ( ) Budgeted as a percentage of expected revenues?
   ( ) Limited to a fixed dollar amount?
   ( ) Some other basis of determination? _____

8. Again, keeping in mind the potential use of Federal funds to construct rapid transit and other capital projects, do you agree or disagree with the following statement from a mass transit report: The statement:
   "Taking into account the symbolic as well as the utilitarian role of the automobile in modern life, we are convinced that any public transit system is almost by definition unattractive to great numbers of residents in the metropolitan area. In the years ahead, there are persuasive reasons to believe that the transit system will only supplement automobile transportation. . . . A few necessity riders will remain, and perhaps others can be persuaded to return. . . . Under

no circumstances, however, can the transit system be made so attractive in comparison with the automobile that a sufficient volume of patronage can be attracted to pay for the costs of operation."
I agree with the statement _____   I disagree with the statement _____

9. Do you agree or disagree with the following statements?

	Agree	*Disagree*
a. Without the profit motive, there is little chance for efficiency.	_____	_____
b. Publicly operated systems subject to a trust indenture have the same profit motives as private companies, except that they don't pay dividends to stockholders.	_____	_____
c. Publicly operated systems *not* subject to a trust indenture tend to be less efficient than private companies or public *subject* to a trust indenture.	_____	_____
d. Present rapid transit (including monorail) technology, if operated in more cities, would reverse present downward patronage trends.	_____	_____
e. Air-conditioned buses operating on freeways (without separate lanes) will be sufficient to reverse adverse traffic trends.	_____	_____
f. Subsidized public systems will find it extremely difficult to resist political pressures with respect to employment.		
g. Labor unions tend to have more strength under public ownership as contrasted with private.	_____	_____
h. Bus rapid transit on freeways without special lanes can be operated in your city and cover all operating costs including depreciation and allocated overhead.	_____	_____

10. Following a fare increase, your company was able to improve its net income position last year. As you evaluate your capital budget, you find that you will have $200,000 to spend on capital improvements that you had *not* counted on. Which of the following would you tend to spend the money on? (Please rank in order)
    ( ) Air condition 44 buses of your fleet of 800.
    ( ) Make improvements in your maintenance facilities.
    ( ) Invest in securities, that is, set up a fund for contingencies.
    ( ) Purchase seven new buses.
    ( ) Increase the advertising budget by $200,000.
    ( ) Use the money to support experimental extensions of service.

11. Your company operates in a city where the maximum temperature during June, July, and August usually exceeds 85 degrees. Although the city is not a "southern" city, it is generally agreed that "during the summer months, it is a pretty uncomfortable place to live." You operate a fleet of 1,000 buses, 200 of which are over 10 years old. Your average operating cost per bus mile is 70 cents. You presently have no air-conditioned buses. Your base service is covered by 400 buses and your peak service uses 950 buses. To air condition the buses would cost $4,500 per unit and increase maintenance and operating costs by 1.75 cents per bus mile. Which of the following would you *most* likely do: (Choose one) (Assume you have adequate borrowing capacity at 4% interest)

( ) Air condition your total fleet of buses.

( ) Air condition the base fleet of 400 buses only.

( ) Use the funds for some other purpose.

Selected Bibliography

A. U.S. Government Publications and Legal Documents

Pennsylvania Railroad Company v. Pennsylvania Public Utility Commission. Record. Superior Court of Pennsylvania, October Term, 1962, No. 153.

U.S. Bureau of the Census, *Special Reports—Street and Electric Railways 1902,* 1905.

U.S. Bureau of the Census, *U.S. Census of Population: 1960 Number of Inhabitants United States Summary.* Final Report PC(1)-1A, 1961.

U.S. Business and Defense Services Administration, Office of Marketing Service, *Changing Metropolitan Markets, 1950–1960,* 1961.

U.S. Congress, House, Committee on Banking and Currency
Hearings, Metropolitan Mass Transportation, 86th Cong., 2d Sess., 1960.
Hearings, Urban Mass Transportation 1961, 87th Cong., 1st Sess., 1961.
Hearings, Urban Mass Transportation Act of 1962, 87th Cong. 2d. Sess., 1962.

U.S. Congress, House, Committee on Ways and Means, *Final Report of the Highway Cost Allocation Study.* Parts I–V, House Document 54. Part VI, House Document 72. 87th Cong. 1st Sess., 1961.

U.S. Congress, House, Committee of the Whole House on the State of the Union, *The Transportation System of Our Nation: Message from the President of the United States.* House Document 384. 87th Cong., 2d Sess., 1962.

U.S. Congress, Joint Committee on Washington Metropolitan Problems *Rapid Transit Systems in Six Metropolitan Areas.* A staff report prepared by Gunther M. Gottfeld. 86th Cong., 1st Sess., 1959.

U.S. Congress, Senate, Committee on Banking and Currency
Hearings, Urban Mass Transportation 1961, 87th Cong., 1st Sess., 1961.
Hearings, Urban Mass Transportation 1962, 87th Cong., 2d Sess., 1962.

Report, Urban Mass Transportation Act of 1963, 88th Cong., 1st Sess., 1963.

Summary of the Provisions of S. 6, the Urban Mass Transportation Act of 1963, As Passed By the Senate on April 4, 1963, 88th Cong., 1st Sess., 1963.

U.S. Congress, Senate, Committee on Commerce
Hearings, Urban Mass Transportation 1963, 88th Cong., 1st Sess., 1963.

U.S. Congress, Senate, Committee on Interstate and Foreign Commerce, *Commuter Transportation*. A report prepared by Anthony Arpaia and the Regional Plan Association, 87th Cong., 1st Sess., 1961.

U.S. Congress, Senate, Committee on Interstate and Foreign Commerce, Special Study Group on Transportation Policies in the United States. *National Transportation Policy: Preliminary Draft of a Report*. 87th Cong., 1st Sess., 1961. (Popularly known as the Doyle Report).

U.S. National Capital Transportation Agency, *Recommendations for Transportation in the National Capital Region*. Washington: G.P.O., 1962.

B. Books, Reports, and Pamphlets

Advisory Commission on Intergovernmental Relations, *Intergovernmental Responsibilities for Mass Transportation Facilities and Services in Metropolitan Areas*. Washington: By the Commission, 1961.

American Municipal Association, *The Collapse of Commuter Service*. Washington: By the Association, 1959.

American Transit Association
Comparative Tabulation of the Features of Public Transit Authorities. New York: American Transit Association, 1958. (Mimeographed)

List of Experiments with Bargain and or Short Haul Fares—Urban Transit Industry. New York: American Transit Association, 1962. (Mimeographed)

Publicly Owned Transit Systems in the United States. New York: American Transit Association, 1961. (Mimeographed)

Transit Faces the Future. New York: American Transit Association, 1959.

Transit Fact Book, Selected Years. New York: American Transit Association, annually.

American Transit Association, Committee on Fare Structures, *Fare Structures in the Transit Industry*. New York: American Transit Association, 1933.

Andrews, Richard D., *Urban Growth and Development*. New York: Simmons-Boardman, 1962.

Association of American Railroads, Bureau of Railway Economics, *Government Expenditures for Construction Operation and Maintenance of Transport Facilities by Air Highway and Waterway and Private Expenditures for Construction Maintenance of Way and Taxes on Railroad Facilities*. Washington: Association of American Railroads, 1964.

Automobile Manufacturers Association, *Automobile Facts and Figures,* 1964 Edition. Detroit: By the Association, 1964.

Bauer, John, and Peter Costello, *Transit Modernization and Street Traffic Control*. Chicago: Public Administration Service, 1950.

Bello, Francis, "The City and the Car," *The Exploding Metropolis*. Ed. the Editors of *Fortune*. Garden City: Doubleday, 1957, pp. 32–61.

Berry, Donald S., George W. Blomme, Paul Shuldiner, and John H. Jones, *The Technology of Urban Transportation*. Chicago: Northwestern University, 1963.

Bone, A. J. and Martin Wohl, *Economic Impact Study of Massachusetts Route 128*. Cambridge: Massachusetts Institute of Technology, 1958.

Botzow, Hermann S. D., Jr., *Monorails*. New York: Simmons Boardman, 1960.

Bowersox, R. L., ed., *America is Going Places*. Erie: General Electric, 1962.

California, University of, Institute of Transportation and Traffic Engineering, *Selected References on Mass Transit*. Berkeley: By the Institute, periodically.

Chicago Area Transportation Study, Vols. I, II, and III. Chicago: Chicago Area Transportation Study, 1959–1962.

Chicago, City of, *Chicago's West Side Subway*. Chicago: By the City, 1958.

Chicago Transit Authority

Analysis of City of Chicago Cordon Counts. Chicago: By the Authority, 1961.

Chicago's Mass Transportation System. Chicago: By the Authority, 1959.

New Horizons for the Chicago Metropolitan Area. Chicago: By the Authority, 1957.

Trend of Passenger Traffic Leaving the Central District During the Peak Evening Hour By Mode of Transportation. Chicago: By the Authority, 1962.

Cleveland, City of, 1961 *Cordon Count.* Cleveland: By the City, 1961.

Cleveland Transit System

    Rapid Transit Extension to Cleveland Hopkins Airport. Cleveland: By the System, 1960.

    Southwest Rapid Transit Extension to Brooklyn-Parma Area. Cleveland: By the System, 1962.

Commonwealth of Massachusetts

    Report of the Joint Special Legislative Committee on Transportation. House of Representatives No. 3400. January 1962.

Commonwealth of Massachusetts, Mass Transportation Commission

    The Boston Region. Prepared by Melvin R. Levin. Boston: By the Commission, 1963.

    The Boston Regional Survey, A Bibliography of Planning Studies. Prepared by the Planning Services Group. Boston: By the Commission, 1962.

    Demonstration Project Progress Report Number 5—Tentative Conclusions. Boston: By the Commission, 1963.

    Mass Transportation in Massachusetts: Final Report on a Mass Transportation Demonstration Project. Boston: By the Commission, 1964.

Conway, Thomas, "Franchises and Public Regulation," *Principles of Urban Transportation,* Ed. Frank H. Mossman. Cleveland: Western Reserve University, 1951, pp. 21–32.

Coverdale & Colpitts, *Report to Los Angeles Metropolitan Transit Authority—A Study of Bus Transportation as a Means of Mass Rapid Transit for Los Angeles.* New York: Coverdale & Colpitts, 1955.

Daniel, Mann, Johnson, and Mendenhall, *Rapid Transit Program.* Los Angeles: Los Angeles Metropolitan Transit Authority, 1960.

Deem, Warren H., *The Problem of Boston's Metropolitan Transit Authority.* Cambridge: Harvard University Graduate School of Public Administration, 1953.

Futterman, Robert, *The Future of Our Cities.* Garden City: Doubleday, 1961.

Gibbs, Donald L. "Problems of the Cities," *Proceedings of the 1961–1962 Series of Citizen Seminars on the Fiscal, Economic, and Political Problems of Boston and the Metropolitan Community.* Chestnut Hill: College of Business Administration, Boston College, 1962, pp. 137–144.

Gottman, Jean, *Megalopolis.* New York: Twentieth Century Fund, 1961.

Grand River Avenue Transit Study, Detroit, Michigan—Summary of Significant Findings. Detroit: Department of Street Railways, 1962.

Greater Boston Economic Study Committee, *A Study of Commuters on the Highland Branch.* Boston: By the Committee, 1960.

Hofstad, Lawrence R., *A Look Ahead in Highway Transportation.* Detroit: General Motors Research Laboratories, 1961.

Hilton, George W., and John F. Due, *The Electric Interurban Railways in America.* Stanford: Stanford University, 1960.

Homburger, Wolfgang S., *A Study of Express Bus Operation on Freeways.* Berkeley: University of California Institute of Transportation and Traffic Engineering, 1956.

Homburger, Wolfgang S., and Norman Kennedy, *The Utilization of Freeways by Urban Transit Buses: A Nationwide Survey.* Berkeley: University of California Institute of Transportation and Traffic Engineering, 1958.

Hyde, Donald C., *The Future of Metropolitan Cleveland Depends on the Downtown Subway.* Cleveland: Cleveland Transit System, 1957.

Institute of Public Administration, *Suburbs to Grand Central: A Study of the Feasibility of Reorganizing the Suburban Services of the New York Central and New Haven Railroads Under a Public Agency.* New York: By the Institute, 1963.

Institute for Rapid Transit, *A Report to The Nation—Proceedings of First Annual Meeting.* Washington: By the Institute, 1962.

Jackson, Dugald, and David J. McGrath, *Street Railway Fares—Their Relation to Length of Haul and Cost of Service.* New York: McGraw-Hill, 1917.

Kennedy, Norman, and Wolfgang S. Homburger, *The Organization of Metropolitan Transit Agencies.* Berkeley: University of California Institute of Transportation and Traffic Engineering, 1961.

Landsberg, Hans H., Leonard L. Fischman, and Joseph L. Fisher, *Resources in America's Future: Patterns of Requirements and Availabilities, 1960–2000.* Baltimore: Johns Hopkins Press for Resources of the Future Inc., 1963.

Lang, A. Scheffer, and Richard M. Soberman, *Urban Rail Transit.* Cambridge: The Joint Center for Urban Studies of the Massachusetts Institute of Technology and Harvard University, 1964.

Los Angeles Metropolitan Transit Authority, *Report on "Backbone" Rapid Transit Route for Los Angeles.* Los Angeles: By the Authority, 1961.

Martin, B. V., F. W. Memmott, and A. J. Bone, *Principles and Techniques of Predicting Future Demand for Urban Area Transportation.* Cambridge: Massachusetts Institute of Technology School of Engineering, 1963.

Metropolitan Rapid Transit Commission, *Metropolitan Rapid Transit Financing.* A Report Prepared by William Miller. New York: By the Commission, 1957.

Meyer, John R., John F. Kain, and Martin Wohl, "Technology and Urban Transportation–A Report Prepared for the White House Panel on Civilian Technology." Cambridge: By the authors, 1962. (Mimeographed). (A later and more complete expression of the viewpoints of these authors can be found in their book, *The Urban Transportation Problem,* to be published by the Harvard University Press in early 1965.)

Miller, John A., *Fares Please.* New York: Dover, 1960.

Mossman, Frank H. (ed.), *Principles of Urban Transportation.* Cleveland: Western Reserve University, 1951.

Moses, Leon, "Economics of Consumer Choice in Urban Transportation," *Proceedings—The Dynamics of Urban Transportation.* Detroit: Automobile Manufacturers Association, 1962, pp. 16–1 through 16–8.

Northwestern University Transportation Center, *Basic Issues in Chicago Metropolitan Transportation.* Chicago: Northwestern University, 1958.

Oi, Walter Y., and Paul Shuldiner, *An Analysis of Urban Travel Demands.* Chicago: Northwestern University, 1962.

Owen, Wilfred, *The Metropolitan Transportation Problem.* Washington: Brookings, 1956.

Paranka, Stephen, *Urban Transportation Dilemma.* Atlanta: Georgia State College of Business Administration, 1961.

Philadelphia, City of, Department of Public Property, *Philadelphia's Capital Program for Transit Operations: 1961–1965.* Philadelphia: By the Department, 1961.

Philadelphia, City of, Mayor's Transit Study Task Force, *The Public Transit Authority—A Study of Five Cities.* Philadelphia: By the City, 1963.

Philadelphia, City of, Urban Traffic & Transportation Board
  Analysis of Operation Northwest. Philadelphia: By the Board, 1960.
  Plan and Program, 1955. Philadelphia: By the Board, 1956.
  UTTB: April 1956–May 1960. Philadelphia: By the Board, 1960.

Pickard, Jerome, *The Metropolitanization of the United States* quoted in *The Human Need for Rapid Transportation*. Mansfield: Ohio Brass, 1960.

Pittsburgh Area Transportation Study, Vols. I and II. Pittsburgh: Pittsburgh Area Transportation Study, 1961–1963.

Pratt, Douglas, *Transit Progress is Linked with City-PTC Cooperation*. Philadelphia: Philadelphia Transportation Company, 1962.

Regional Plan Association, *Hub Bound Travel in the Tri-State Metropolitan Region*. New York: By the Association, 1961.

Reinsberg, Mark, *Growth and Change in Metropolitan Areas and Their Relation to Metropolitan Transportation—A Research Summary*. Chicago: Northwestern University, 1961.

Rowsome, Frank, Jr., *Trolley Car Treasury*. New York: McGraw-Hill, 1956.

Schroeder, Werner W., *Metropolitan Transit Research*. Chicago: Chicago Transit Authority, 1956.

Seminar Research Bureau, Boston College. *Studies of Urban Transportation, Travel in the Boston Region, 1959–1980*. Chestnut Hill: Boston College, 1960–1961.

Smith, Wilbur & Associates, *Future Highways and Urban Growth*. New Haven: Wilbur Smith & Associates, 1961.

Sternlieb, George, *The Future of the Downtown Department Store*. Cambridge: Joint Center for Urban Studies, Massachusetts Institute of Technology and Harvard University, 1962.

Taafe, Edward J., Barry J. Garner, and Maurice H. Yeats, *The Peripheral Journey to Work: A Geographic Consideration*. Chicago: Northwestern University, 1963.

Transit Advertising Association, Inc., *The Transit Millions*. Prepared by Sindlinger & Company. New York: By the Association, 1964.

Warner, Stanley L., *Stochastic Choice of Mode in Urban Travel: A Study in Binary Choice*. Chicago: Northwestern University, 1962.

Westinghouse Industrial Systems, *The Westinghouse Transit Expressway*. Pittsburgh: Westinghouse, 1962.

Williams, Harry A., *Just Who is Trying to Ruin Our Cities?* Detroit: Automobile Manufacturers Association, 1962.

Young, Dallas M., *Twentieth-Century Experience in Urban Transit: A Study of the Cleveland System*. Cleveland: Western Reserve University, 1960.

Zettel, Richard M., and Richard R. Carll, *Summary Review of Major Metropolitan Area Transportation Studies in the United States*. Berkeley: University of California Institute of Transportation and Traffic Engineering, 1962.

C.   General References

Annual Reports
  Chicago Transit Authority
  Cleveland Transit System
  Los Angeles Metropolitan Transit Authority
  Metropolitan Transit Authority (Boston)
  New York City Transit Authority
  Passenger Service Improvement Corporation (Philadelphia)
  Philadelphia Transportation Company
  Saint Louis Public Service Company
Boston Globe
Boston Herald
Business Week
Cleveland Plain Dealer
Cleveland Press
Congressional Quarterly Weekly Report
General Electric Company, *Going Places*
Institute for Rapid Transit, *Newsletter*
Metropolitan Transportation (*Modern Passenger Transportation,* December 1959–January 1961, and *Mass Transportation* prior to December, 1959).
Moody's Municipal and Government Manual
Moody's Transportation Manual
New York Times
Passenger Transport
Railway Age
Survey of Current Business, July 1962
Trains

D.   Articles and Papers

Anderson, George, "Rail and Bus Rapid Transit for Downtown Access," *Proceedings—The Dynamics of Urban Transportation.* Detroit: Automobile Manufacturers Association, 1962, pp. 7–1 through 7–15.

Burck, Gilbert, "How to Unchoke Our Cities," *Fortune,* LXIII (May 1961), pp. 119–123, 256–264.

Cleave, Walter C., "Mechanical Fare Collection," *Metropolitan Transportation,* LIII (December 1957), pp. 20–22.

Conway, Thomas, Jr., "1950–1960 Population Shift Poses Transportation Problem," *Traffic Quarterly,* XV (January 1961), pp. 62–85.

Dichter, Ernest, "The World Customer," *Harvard Business Review,* 40 (July–August 1962), pp. 113–122.

Ditmar, Paul, "Letter to the Editor," *Metropolitan Transportation,* LVIII (February 1962), p. 11.

Doody, Francis S., "The Economics of Toll Roads," *Traffic Quarterly,* XVI (October 1962), pp. 469–487.

Hilton, George W., "The Decline of Railroad Commutation," *Business History Review,* XXXVI (Summer 1962), pp. 171–187.

Jones, Paul S., and John L. Crain, "The $10 Billion Transit Market If . . . ," *Metropolitan Transportation,* LX (January 1964), pp. 16–18.

Malo, Alger F., "The Relation of Mass Transportation to Total Transportation in Detroit," *Traffic Quarterly,* XV (April 1961), pp. 226–247.

Maloney, Joseph, "The Massachusetts Approach to Regional Planning," *Traffic Quarterly,* XVI (October 1962), pp. 614–632.

McMillan, Samuel C., "Changing Position of Retail Trade in Central Business Districts," *Traffic Quarterly,* XI (July 1957), pp. 75–94.

——, "Recent Trends in the Decentralization of Retail Trade," *Traffic Quarterly,* XVI (January 1962), pp. 75–94.

Myers, Edward T., "Urban Transit: The Pendulum Swings Back," *Modern Railroads,* XVII (May 1962), pp. 61–77.

Palmer, Foster, "The Literature of the Street Railway," *Harvard Library Bulletin,* XII (Winter 1958), pp. 117–138.

"Penn-Jersey Transportation Study," *P-J News,* August–September 1962.

Quinby, Henry D., "The Rapid Transit District Project of the San Francisco Bay Area," *Traffic Quarterly,* XV (April 1961), pp. 352–370.

"Roads for 1975's Traffic," *Business Week,* June 16, 1962, pp. 54–60.

Roberts, Sidney I., "Portrait of a Robber Baron: Charles T. Yerkes," *Business History Review,* XXXV (Autumn 1961), pp. 344–371.

Saunders, William B., "How Automated Planning Can Be Programmed," *Metropolitan Transportation,* LVIII (March 1962), pp. 18–23.

Schmandt, Henry J. and G. Ross Stephens, "Public Transportation and the Worker," *Traffic Quarterly,* XVII (October 1963), pp. 573–583.

Schneider, Lewis M., "Impact of Rapid Transit Extensions on Suburban Bus Companies," *Traffic Quarterly,* XV (January 1961), pp. 135–152.

Schnore, Leo, "The Use of Public Transportation in Urban Areas," *Traffic Quarterly,* XVI (October 1962), pp. 499–509.

Smith, R. Gilman, "Coordinated Transport Planning for the St. Louis Area," *Traffic Quarterly,* XIV (April 1960), pp. 143–160.

"Tide Turns for Transit," *Business Week,* October 20, 1962, pp. 77–88.

Vernon, Raymond, "The Economics and Finances of the Large Metropolis," *Daedelus,* XC (Winter 1961), pp. 31–47.

Wilson, Robert S., "Transit on Credit," *Metropolitan Transportation,* LIII (August 1957), pp. 23.

E.   Unpublished Material

Levine, Julius S., "Impact and Implications of the MTA's Highland Branch Extension for the Boston Metropolitan Area." Unpublished Master's dissertation, Massachusetts Institute of Technology, 1960.

Statement of Robert Stier, President of Philadelphia Transportation Company, to Philadelphia City Council Subcommittee on Transportation dated April 30, 1962. (Processed)

Statement of Merritt H. Taylor, Jr., President of Philadelphia Suburban Transportation Company (Red Arrow Lines) before Delaware County Commissioners' Hearing re SEPACT, 1962. (Processed)

Statement of Austin J. Tobin, Executive Director of The Port of New York Authority, dated August 30, 1962. (Mimeographed)

Wilson, Robert J., "An Analysis of Transit Coach Air Conditioning." Unpublished report, General Motors Institute, 1962.

Index